Cooking Without Your Salt Shaker

AMERICAN HEART ASSOCIATION NORTHEAST OHIO AFFILIATE, INC.
in cooperation with the Cleveland Dietetic Association

Acknowledgments

The American Heart Association acknowledges the Northeast Ohio Affiliate's Low Sodium Cookbook Task Force for the development of *Cooking Without Your Salt Shaker.* Special recognition is accorded Sharon Reichman, R.D., who chaired the task force and Charlene Krejci, R.D., Karen Wilcoxon Izso, R.D., Grace Petot, R.D., and Sally Gleason, R.D. Other task force members included Tab Forgac, R.D., Rosemary Manni, R.D., Auretha Pettigrew, R.D., Robert Post, M.D., and Mary Ann Weber, R.D. Appreciation is also expressed to the Diet Therapy Section of the Cleveland Dietetic Association and especially to those people who offered suggestions and tested recipes.

Table of Contents

NOTE TO DOCTOR AND DIETITIAN:
This cookbook is for the person who must mildly restrict salt or sodium intake. However, the recipes can easily be adapted to a specific lower level of sodium to correspond with your diet instruction.

Welcome to our cookbook

Eating is a subject on which most people consider themselves experts — because they've been doing it all their lives! Yet, many of us have been consuming too much sodium, too much fat and the wrong kind of fat. If you would like to cut down on the amount of sodium and fat in your diet or if your doctor has suggested a "low-salt," modified fat diet, then you'll find this cookbook an excellent guide. If your doctor has given you specific instructions, you may still use the recipes in this book by adapting them to your own diet.

The why's and wherefore's of salt and sodium. To get down to basics, we need to understand what sodium is and the difference between salt and sodium. We all know what salt is. Sodium, however, is a mineral found in nature and in almost all the food we eat. It is not the same as salt. Salt is nearly half sodium and most of the sodium we eat comes from ordinary salt used in cooking or at the table. Confused? You needn't be.

Everyone needs some sodium to live. However, our need for sodium can be met without using salt because sodium is found naturally in so many foods. One of the most common reasons a doctor recommends cutting down on salt or sodium in the diet is to control high blood pressure. This is important because high blood pressure increases the risk of heart attack, stroke and kidney failure. There are many other reasons a doctor may advise decreasing salt or sodium intake. While the scientific evidence is not conclusive, studies show that it may be wise for all of us to cut down on our salt intake. For these reasons, none of the recipes in this cookbook contain added salt.

What about fat and cholesterol? In addition to lowering the sodium in your food, recipes and recommended numbers of servings have been chosen for this cookbook with a fat-modified, low-cholesterol diet in mind. The Heart Association recommends decreasing your intake of fat-laden and cholesterol-rich foods and also changing the kinds of fat you use. There are two kinds of fat you should be especially concerned about: polyunsaturated and saturated. As you continue reading these pages, you will learn how to use polyunsaturated fats and how to decrease the saturated fat in your diet.

You may also be pleasantly surprised to know that by cutting down on fats in your food and serving slightly smaller portions, you will be taking in fewer calories. An approximate calorie content for one serving accompanies each recipe.

In summary. By reducing the amount of sodium in your foods, changing the kind of fat and decreasing the amount of fat and cholesterol in your diet, the American

Heart Association believes you can help
reduce your risk of developing heart
disease. At first, you may find it
difficult to modify eating habits and
change some cooking methods that you have
followed for many years. The first step is
to take the salt shaker off the table. Then
use this cookbook. It can help you.
Remember that it is not intended to take
the place of your doctor's instruction.
Should you have any questions, ask your
doctor or call your local Heart Association.
  Happy cooking!

*IF YOU HAVE RECEIVED A LOW-SODIUM DIET
INSTRUCTION FROM YOUR DOCTOR OR DIETITIAN . . .
check your diet instruction against the recipe ingredients. To help you
select the appropriate foods, some recipe ingredients are marked with an
asterisk (*). These foods are available in an unsalted form. Follow the
recipes using ingredients without salt only when they are specified in
your diet instruction sheet. All recipes have been tested with unsalted
ingredients.

When You Go Shopping

When you go shopping

A diet lower in sodium can still taste good and be nutritionally complete. The key is to select a variety of foods which promote good health. Your daily food choices should include:

- no more than 6 ounces of lean meat, fish or poultry
- use dried beans, peas, lentils or soybean curd (tofu) in place of meat a few times a week
- use whole grain or enriched bread or cereal products
- 3 or more servings of fruit or 3 or more servings of vegetables (include 1 serving of citrus fruit or vegetable high in vitamin C and 1 serving of dark green, leafy or deep yellow vegetables)
- 2 or more servings of skim milk or low-fat milk products for adults; 3 to 4 servings for children or adolescents
- 5-8 servings of polyunsaturated and monounsaturated fats and oils in the form of margarine, cooking oil and unsalted salad dressing

With a little effort, you can learn to decrease the sodium, change the kind of fat and reduce the amount of fat and cholesterol in your diet. Begin with the recipes in this book. Then, adapt your own favorite recipes by omitting the salt and using the ingredient substitutions listed on page 15. To save time later you may wish to consider doubling the quantity of a recipe and freezing the unused portion.

Spices, herbs and other flavorings add zest to a recipe and should be used instead of salt. Be adventurous and try some new flavor ideas. You may also want to ask your doctor about using a salt substitute. If it is allowed, use it sparingly at the table, since salt substitutes tend to be bitter when used heavily.

Most of the recipe ingredients called for in this cookbook are readily available in your local grocery store. Some, such as unsalted tomato paste and tomato puree, will be found in the usual section of the grocery store. Other unsalted foods can be found in a special diet section. If they are not in stock, your grocer can probably order them for you.

Meat and other protein foods For a balanced diet, everyone should eat some protein foods every day. To reduce your salt intake, these foods should include only unsalted fresh, frozen or canned lean meat, fish or poultry. Because even these contain cholesterol, it is especially important that they be limited to 6 ounces per day. All meats contain fat, but fish, poultry and veal contain smaller amounts of fat and should be eaten more frequently than other kinds of meat. By carefully selecting the meat you buy and

4

by substituting other protein foods for meat, you can further reduce the fat in your diet.

Dried beans, dried peas, soybeans, peanut butter and unsalted nuts may be substituted for meat or used as meat extenders. Dry cottage cheese made without added salt is another good substitute for meat because it is also low in fat. Most other cheeses contain significant amounts of salt, saturated fat and cholesterol. Although it is difficult to find cheese which is low in fat and also unsalted, you may be able to find a local dairy which makes it.

Surprisingly enough, egg whites may be used as a substitute for meat. Although egg yolks contain very large amounts of cholesterol, the whites contain neither cholesterol nor fat and may be used as often as you like. The American Heart Association recommends that you use no more than 3 egg yolks per week, including those used in cooking or baking. The recipe for No-Cholesterol Egg Substitute on page 37 may be used as a substitute for some of your favorite egg dishes.

Shopping for meat The best meats for you are those lean cuts that have less fat around the outside and less marbled fat throughout the meat. Your butcher will be glad to help you select the leanest cuts.

The selection of ground beef deserves your special attention. Again, the leanest meat available is the best for you. A medium-to-bright red color signifies a low fat content, while a light pink color indicates that excess fat has been ground in with the meat. An even better idea is to select a lean cut of meat and ask the butcher to trim it and grind it for you. This is usually done at no extra charge.

When selecting chicken, remember that broilers and fryers are preferable because they contain the least amount of fat.

We do **not** recommend the following meats and fish for frequent use because they contain large amounts of sodium, fat and/or cholesterol:

luncheon meats
frankfurters
sausage
spareribs
corned beef
liver and other
  organ meats
shrimp
smoked, cured or dried fish and
  meats including bacon and ham
canned meat, fish or
  poultry, unless packed
  without salt

Milk and Milk Products Everyone should have two or more servings of skim milk (0-1% milk fat) or low-fat milk products every day. Although milk and most milk products do not contain added salt (with the exception of buttermilk and cheese), whole milk and products made from it contain significant amounts of cholesterol and saturated fats and should be avoided. Products from the following list can be substituted for whole milk products and are recommended because they are lower in fat and cholesterol. You'll want to choose products fortified with vitamins A and D.

- skim milk, evaporated skim milk, non-fat dry milk
- dry cottage cheese which has no salt added
- cheese made from skim or partially skim milk with no salt added (no more than 2 grams of fat per ounce)
- low-fat yogurt or low-fat frozen yogurt
- ice milk and sherbets
- polyunsaturated non-dairy creamers or whiteners (Imitation sour cream, whipped topping and other non-dairy coffee whiteners contain saturated fat and are not recommended.)

Fruits and Vegetables Everyone should have at least three servings of fruits and vegetables daily, including one serving of citrus fruit or vegetable high in vitamin C and one serving of a dark green leafy or deep yellow vegetable.

Fruit is great because it contains practically no sodium, no cholesterol and, except for the avocado, no fat. Fruits are low in calories and add vitamins, minerals and fiber to the diet. Plus, they make excellent snacks! Eat any kind of fruit or juice you like – fresh, frozen, canned or dried.

Vegetables are also good for you because they contain no fat or cholesterol. Fresh vegetables and most frozen ones contain very little sodium and may be eaten as desired. You really should avoid buying canned or frozen vegetables that contain added salt, butter or sauces, but if you enjoy canning or freezing vegetables at home, you can get excellent results by leaving out the salt and following the usual processing directions. Vegetables which have been pickled or packed in brine, such as pickles or sauerkraut, contain extremely large amounts of salt and should not be eaten.

Breads and cereal products Your balanced diet should include whole grain or enriched bread or cereal products. There are so many different kinds of bread on the market that it's really fun to experiment. Breads such as white, whole or cracked wheat, rye, French, Italian, pumpernickel and plain rolls are perfectly acceptable for you to eat although they contain some sodium and small amounts of fat. Soda crackers that don't have salt sprinkled on the top, matzo, melba toast and bread sticks also contain small amounts of sodium and fat but they, too, are acceptable and can be included in your diet. Most other crackers contain large amounts of sodium and fat and you would be wise to avoid them.

Commercial baked goods and mixes for muffins, biscuits, sweet rolls, cakes, cookies and pastries contain significant amounts of sodium and/or cholesterol and saturated fat. It would be much better to bake your own. You can either use the recipes in this cookbook or adjust your own favorite recipes by omitting the salt and using the ingredient substitutions on page 15.

Cereals can be great for people trying to follow a lower-sodium, fat-modified diet. Most do not contain saturated fat or cholesterol. Read the label and choose only those which contain recommended fats, pages 7 & 8. Many cold cereals and instant hot cereals do contain some sodium, but they may be used in your diet. Other hot cereals as well as rice and pastas, such as spaghetti and macaroni, contain practically no sodium and are certainly acceptable; but do remember to omit the salt from the cooking water when preparing these foods.

Fats and oils Polyunsaturated and monounsaturated fats and oils are important elements in your daily diet. Five to eight servings of polyunsaturated and monounsaturated fats and oils should be used daily. This can be in the form of unsalted salad dressing or margarine or oil used in cooking. Oils are cholesterol-free and do not contain sodium. although low in cholesterol, mayonnaise and most margarines do contain some salt, but they are still acceptable for use. Other commercial salad dressings should be avoided because they contain large amounts of salt.

It is generally agreed that we all eat too much fat. It is, however, important to make changes not only in the amount of fat but in the kind of fat eaten. The chart below lists those fats which are recommended and those which are not recommended.

Recommended Vegetable Oils
safflower oil
corn oil
cottonseed oil
soybean oil
sesame seed oil
sunflower seed oil
canola
olive oil
polyunsaturated margarine
mayonnaise
unsalted salad dressing

Not Recommended/Saturated
butter
vegetable shortening
vegetable fat
bacon, salt pork
suet, lard
chicken fat, meat fat
coconut oil
hydrogenated vegetable oil
palm kernel oil
palm oil

For occasional use only:
peanut oil

What is a polyunsaturated margarine? Read the label to decide.

SAMPLE LABEL

BRAND X POLYUNSATURATED MARGARINE
Nutrition Information Per Serving

Serving size	14 grams (about 1 tbsp.)
Servings per container	32 (per pound container)
Calories	100
Protein	0
Carbohydrate	0
Fat	11 grams
Percent of calories from fat	over 99%
Polyunsaturated	4 grams
Saturated	2 grams
Cholesterol	0 (0 per 100 grams)

Here is how to use this information. Look at the amount of polyunsaturated and saturated fats:

If the margarine contains	**Then it is**
At least twice as much polyunsaturated as saturated fat	Recommended
Less than twice as much polyunsaturated as saturated fat	Not Recommended

To determine if the margarine is recommended or not recommended, divide the number of grams of polyunsaturated fat by the number of grams of saturated fat. If the answer is 2 or higher, the margarine is recommended.

If a margarine does not contain a nutrition label, look for one that does. Manufacturers occasionally change product ingredients so read the label each time you select a product — even if it's one you've used before. Label-reading can be helpful with many other products, too!

Beverages The following beverages are satisfactory for use since they contain insignificant amounts of fat or cholesterol and little or no sodium: water, skim milk, fruit juices, fruit drinks, coffee, tea, carbonated beverages, beer, table wine and alcohol.

However, if you are trying to lose weight and need to limit calories, you may wish to avoid those beverages which give you calories without giving you nutritional value. Such drinks include: sugared carbonated beverages and fruit drinks, beer, wine and alcohol.

Miscellaneous foods and flavorings

Many commonly used commercial seasonings and sauces contain significant amounts of sodium or salt and should not be used. These include flavorings such as soy sauce, Worcestershire sauce, steak sauce, catsup, chili sauce, monosodium glutamate, meat tenderizer, flavored seasoning salts and bouillon cubes. Commercial soups, olives, relishes, pickles and many snack foods also contain large amounts of salt and should not be used. Some of these products are made without salt and are available commercially. Recipes are provided in this cookbook for catsup, chili sauce, soups, relish and pickles.

Two common food ingredients which should be avoided because of their saturated fat content include chocolate candy and cocoa butter found in baking chocolate and chocolate chips. Unsweetened cocoa powder, however, may be used because most of the fat has been removed.

Flavor Adventures

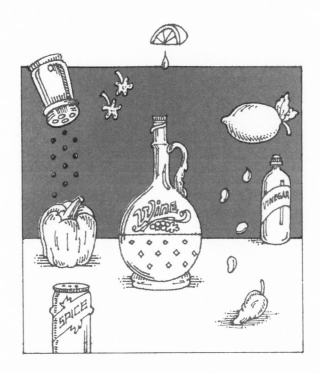

Flavor Adventures

Because most herbs, spices and table wines do not contain sodium, cholesterol or fat, they can be used in place of salt as seasonings. You will find that flavoring substances such as black pepper, onion, green pepper, garlic, lemon juice and vinegar complement and enhance the natural goodness of food. A word of caution, however, when using herbs and spices: use them sparingly because a little goes a long way. **Remember, however, if you use fresh rather than dried herbs, use twice the amount.**

To keep a ready supply of seasonings on hand, try using a combination of herbs instead of salt in your salt shaker. You can make your own herb shaker by combining one-half teaspoon of cayenne pepper, one tablespoon of garlic powder and one teaspoon of each of the following ground seasonings: basil, marjoram, thyme, parsley, savory, mace, onion powder, black pepper and sage. You'll find this combination of flavors a delightful enhancer of meats and vegetables in the kitchen or on the table.

Table wines are fine to use in cooking but avoid flavoring your meats with "cooking wines" as they contain added salt. As with herbs, a little wine goes a long way. You can devise your own flavorful marinades by using wine, vinegar and oil or unsalted salad dressings. Lemon juice, vinegar, hot pepper sauce or unsalted liquid smoke are also great for added flavor to meats, soups and vegetables.

You'll find the following chart an excellent guide for flavor combinations:

Meat & Fish & Poultry		
	Beef:	Bay leaf, dry mustard powder, green pepper, marjoram, fresh mushrooms, nutmeg, onion, pepper, sage, thyme.
	Chicken:	Green pepper, lemon juice, marjoram, fresh mushrooms, paprika, parsley, poultry seasoning, sage, thyme.
	Fish:	Bay leaf, curry powder, dry mustard powder, green pepper, lemon juice, marjoram, fresh mushrooms, paprika.
	Lamb:	Curry powder, garlic, mint, mint jelly, pineapple, rosemary.
	Pork:	Apple, applesauce, garlic, onion, sage.
	Veal:	Apricot, bay leaf, curry powder, ginger, marjoram, oregano.

Vegetables

Asparagus:	Garlic, lemon juice, onion, vinegar.
Corn:	Green pepper, pimiento, fresh tomato.
Cucumbers:	Chives, dill, garlic, vinegar.
Green Beans:	Dill, lemon juice, marjoram, nutmeg, pimiento.
Greens:	Onion, pepper, vinegar.
Peas:	Green pepper, mint, fresh mushrooms, onion, parsley.
Potatoes:	Green pepper, mace, onion, paprika, parsley.
Rice:	Chives, green pepper, onion, pimiento, saffron.
Squash:	Brown sugar, cinnamon, ginger, mace, nutmeg, onion.
Tomatoes:	Basil, marjoram, onion, oregano.

Soup

Soups:	A pinch of dry mustard powder in bean soup; allspice, a small amount of vinegar or a dash of sugar in vegetable soup; peppercorns in skim milk chowders; bay leaf and parsley in pea soup.

Ingredient Substitutions

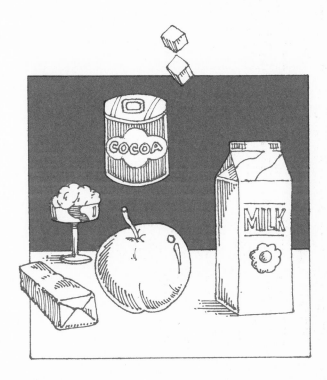

Ingredient Substitutions: Many of your favorite recipes **can** be adjusted for use in your sodium-, fat- and cholesterol-controlled diet without giving up good flavor. To do this, read the ingredients in your recipes carefully and make the appropriate following substitutions as suggested. Unless otherwise indicated, use an equal amount of the substituted ingredient.

Reducing the Sodium Content

If your recipe calls for:	Use:
Broth or bouillon	Unsalted bouillon cubes according to package directions or Beef Broth, page 81, or Chicken Broth, page 82.
Tomato juice	Unsalted tomato juice or dilute one 6-ounce can of unsalted tomato paste with 3 cans of water.
Tomato puree	Unsalted tomato puree or combine one 6-ounce can of unsalted tomato paste with 1 can of water.
Salt	See Flavor Adventures, page 11.
Flavored salts such as onion salt, celery salt and garlic salt.	Onion or garlic powder or celery seed or flakes as indicated in the recipe or according to your preference.

Reducing the Cholesterol and Fat Content

If your recipe calls for:	Use:
Butter, shortening	Margarine (stick form is best for baking).
Melted butter or shortening	Vegetable oil or melted margarine.
Cream cheese	Mock Cream Cheese, page 46.
Baking chocolate	3 tablespoons of unsweetened cocoa powder plus 1 tablespoon of vegetable oil in place of each 1-ounce square of chocolate.
Ice cream	Ice milk, fruit ice, sherbet or low-fat frozen yogurt.

Sour cream, imitation sour cream	Mock Sour Cream, page 84, for cold dishes only. Drained, low-fat plain yogurt for hot and cold foods. (To drain yogurt, line a strainer with a clean cloth, paper towel or a double layer of cheese cloth. Place yogurt in strainer and allow to stand for 30 minutes.)
Whipped cream, non-dairy whipped topping	Mock Whipped Cream, page 108.
Cream	Polyunsaturated coffee creams, undiluted evaporated skim milk, double-strength reconstituted non-fat dry milk powder or skim milk.
Whole eggs	No-Cholesterol Egg Substitute, page 37, or 1 egg white plus 1 teaspoon vegetable oil (which may require some experimenting with baked goods) or commercial cholesterol-free egg substitutes according to package directions.
Milk	Skim milk, reconstituted non-fat dry milk powder or reconstituted evaporated skim milk.
Evaporated milk	Evaporated skim milk.

Entrees and Accompaniments

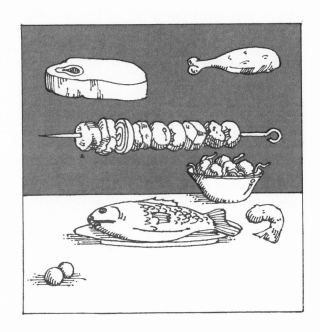

Entrees and Accompaniments

Once you have selected the right kinds of meats for your diet, page 5, you can further reduce the amount of saturated fat by preparing and cooking them according to the following methods.

For beef, pork, lamb and veal, cut off all visible fat surrounding the meat before cooking. To eliminate excess fat from poultry, remove the skin before cooking. Fish does not need special preparation since it is naturally lower in saturated fat.

Less tender cuts of meat may be made more tender before cooking by marinating and/or cooking in a liquid or using an unseasoned meat tenderizer. A tasty marinade might include vinegar, lemon juice or table wine mixed with oil and your favorite herbs and spices. Refrigerate and allow the meat to marinate in a covered container for 12-24 hours, then follow the cooking suggestions below.

Roasting or Baking Flavor meats by rubbing them with your favorite herbs and spices before cooking. Then place meat on a rack in a pan so that the fat drips away and is not absorbed by the meat. Meats should be roasted at a low temperature (325°F.) to reduce shrinkage. Instead of basting the meat with fatty drippings from the pan, use table wine, fruit juices, unsalted broth, vegetable oil or margarine.

Whole chicken or turkey may be roasted with onions, carrots or your favorite vegetables placed inside. The bird will absorb the flavor; however, the vegetables should be discarded after roasting. If you like stuffing with your chicken or turkey, bake it in a separate pan, because dressing or vegetables roasted inside poultry will absorb much of the fat that should drip away during the roasting process.

Broiling To flavor meats or fish for broiling, marinate or rub with garlic or your favorite herbs and spices. Broiling meat on a rack will allow the fat to drip off during cooking. You can also broil fish, but place it in a shallow pan rather than on a rack. To keep meats and fish from drying out during broiling, brush them with vegetable oil, margarine, table wine, fruit juice or a marinade of your own creation.

Braising In preparing meats for braising, you may wish to dust the meat with flour and brown it in vegetable oil or margarine. Then you can add a small amount of water or table wine along with herbs or spices and simmer covered until the meat is tender. If you like gravy, you may follow the method described below for making low-fat gravy.

Gravy As a base, use the broth or juices obtained from cooking the meat or poultry. Skim off excess fat. Chill the broth and remove the hardened fat. If you're in a hurry, add ice cubes to the juices; as they melt, the fat will harden and can be easily removed with a spoon. The remaining liquid should then be heated. You can also add onion or garlic powder or herbs and thicken with flour or cornstarch mixed with a little cold water.

Frying Frying foods is not recommended because foods absorb too much fat this way. For those occasional times when you must fry foods, use vegetable oils instead of solid shortenings. Fish, or meat trimmed of visible fat, may be floured and breaded before frying. Dip the floured meat or fish in skim milk or an egg white and water mixture before coating with herbs and bread crumbs.

Beef Bourguignon

Makes 9 servings

Calories: 210 per serving

2	pounds lean beef chuck, well-trimmed, cut into cubes
¼	cup all-purpose flour
⅛	teaspoon pepper
2	tablespoons oil
½	cup chopped onion
1	garlic clove, minced
¼	teaspoon thyme
¼	teaspoon basil
¼	teaspoon oregano
⅛	teaspoon rosemary
⅛	teaspoon marjoram
1	tablespoon chopped parsley
½	cup dry red table wine
1	cup water
2	cups finely-chopped fresh tomatoes
2	cups diced raw carrots
3	cups diced raw potatoes

Coat beef with flour and pepper. Brown meat in oil. Add onion and garlic, and cook until tender. Pour off fat. Add thyme, basil, oregano, rosemary, marjoram, parsley, wine and water. Cover and simmer 1 hour, stirring occasionally, adding more water if necessary. Add tomatoes and simmer 1 additional hour. Add carrots and potatoes. Simmer 30 minutes.

Peppered Roast Beef

Makes 18 servings

Calories: 160 per serving

5 pounds beef round roast, well-trimmed
2 tablespoons oil
1 teaspoon ground or coarsely-ground pepper

1 medium onion, sliced
1 medium carrot, sliced
1 large stalk celery, sliced
½ cup dry red table wine

Rub meat with oil and pepper and place in an open roasting pan. Insert meat thermometer so bulb reaches center of thickest part. Arrange onion, carrot and celery slices around meat. Pour red wine over all. Roast uncovered in 350°F. oven for 1½ hours or until meat thermometer registers desired degree of doneness. If more liquid is needed, baste with additional wine during the roasting period. Do not use drippings from the roast for basting. Skim fat from pan juices or remove juices with bulb baster and discard fat. Spoon pan juices over thinly sliced meat.

Marinated Beef Slices

Makes 4 servings

Calories: 230 per serving

1 pound lean beef sirloin, well-trimmed, sliced very thin
½ cup lemon juice
2 tablespoons oil
1 cup thinly-sliced fresh mushrooms

½ cup chopped green onions and tops
½ cup thinly-sliced green pepper
¼ teaspoon pepper

Marinate beef in lemon juice for 10 minutes. While meat is marinating, heat oil in large skillet and add mushrooms, onions and green pepper. Cook until onion and green pepper are tender. Remove vegetables from skillet and keep warm. Drain meat, reserving lemon juice marinade. Place meat slices in skillet and brown. Return vegetables to skillet. Add reserved lemon juice and pepper. Heat through. May be served over rice.

Rolled Flank Steak With Bread Dressing

Makes 6 servings

Calories: 330 per serving

1½   pounds flank steak, well-trimmed
½   cup red wine vinegar

1   recipe Bread Dressing, page 31
3   tablespoons oil
½   cup water

Marinate steak in vinegar for 2-3 hours in refrigerator. Turn meat over several times. Drain. Place bread dressing in center of steak and spread to edges. Roll meat, jelly roll fashion, and tie with string. Brown rolled steak in oil in heavy skillet or dutch oven. Pour off fat. Add water, cover and bake in 350°F. oven for 1½ hours or until meat is tender.

Beef Stroganoff

Makes 5 servings

Calories: 265 per serving

1   pound beef tenderloin or sirloin steak, ½-inch thick, well-trimmed
⅛   teaspoon pepper
½   pound fresh mushrooms, sliced
1   medium onion, sliced
3   tablespoons oil
3   tablespoons all-purpose flour
2   unsalted beef bouillon cubes

2   cups boiling water
2   tablespoons unsalted tomato paste
1   teaspoon dry mustard powder
⅛   teaspoon oregano
⅛   teaspoon dill weed
2   tablespoons dry table sherry
⅓   cup low-fat plain yogurt, drained, as directed on page 17

Cut meat into thin strips about 2 inches long. Sprinkle with pepper and set aside. In a large skillet, cook mushrooms and onions in oil. Remove mushrooms and onions and set aside. Place meat strips in same skillet and lightly brown on all sides. Remove meat and set aside. Mix flour into oil in skillet. Dissolve bouillon cubes in boiling water. Gradually add bouillon and simmer, stirring constantly until thickened. Add tomato paste, mustard powder, oregano, dill weed and sherry. Stir. Add beef, mushrooms and onions. Cover tightly and simmer 2-3 minutes or until beef has reached desired degree of doneness. Five minutes before serving, stir in yogurt; heat, but do not boil. May be served over rice.

Miniature Meatballs

Makes 4 servings

Calories: 280 per serving

- 1 pound lean ground beef
- ½ cup dry bread crumbs*
- ¼ teaspoon pepper
- 2 tablespoons oil
- 1 garlic clove
- ½ cup chopped onion

- 1 can (6 ounces) unsalted tomato paste
- 1½ cups water
- 1 teaspoon sugar
- ½ teaspoon basil
- ¼ teaspoon pepper
- ¼ teaspoon oregano

Combine ground beef, bread crumbs and ¼ teaspoon pepper. Shape into 24 small meatballs. Place meatballs on a rack and bake uncovered in 425°F. oven 20 minutes or until meatballs are brown. Cook onion and garlic in oil. Add remaining ingredients except for meatballs. Stir well. Add meatballs, cover and simmer over low heat for 1 hour, stirring occasionally. Remove garlic. Serve over cooked spaghetti for a main dish or spear with toothpicks as an appetizer.

Chili

Makes 6 servings

Calories: 205 per serving

- ¾ cup dried kidney beans
- 3 cups water
- 1 pound lean ground beef
- ½ cup chopped onion
- ½ chopped green pepper
- 1 can (1 pound) tomatoes*, chopped
- 1 can (6 ounces) unsalted tomato paste

- ¾ cup water
- 1 tablespoon chili powder*
- ½ teaspoon oregano
- ¼ teaspoon garlic powder
- ⅛ teaspoon pepper
- 1 bay leaf

Place beans and water in a saucepan. Bring to a boil and cook for 2 minutes. Set aside for one hour without draining. Return beans to heat and simmer for 1 hour or until beans are tender. Drain beans and set aside. Brown ground beef, onion and green pepper together. Pour off fat. Add kidney beans and remaining ingredients. Simmer over low heat 1½ hours, stirring occasionally. Remove bay leaf before serving.

*See page 2

Meatloaf

Makes 6 servings

Calories: 135 per serving

½ cup skim milk
2 slices bread*, broken into pieces
1 pound lean ground beef
2 egg whites, slightly beaten
½ cup chopped onion
2 teaspoons chopped celery
1 medium fresh tomato, peeled and chopped

2 tablespoons unsalted catsup
1 tablespoon lemon juice
⅛ teaspoon pepper
⅛ teaspoon dry mustard powder
⅛ teaspoon sage
⅛ teaspoon garlic powder

Pour milk over bread and allow to stand 5 minutes. Mix in remaining ingredients. Form into a loaf and place on a rack in a shallow roasting pan. Bake in 375°F. oven 1½ hours.

Fantastic Beef Goulash

Makes 6 servings

Calories: 225 per serving

1 cup uncooked macaroni
1 pound lean ground beef
½ pound fresh mushrooms, sliced
1 cup chopped onion
1 garlic clove, minced
1 can (6 ounces) unsalted tomato paste

¾ cup water
1 cup unsalted catsup
1 small bay leaf
1 teaspoon sugar
½ teaspoon pepper
¼ teaspoon oregano
¼ teaspoon basil

Cook macaroni as directed on package, omitting salt. Drain and set aside. Brown ground beef with mushrooms, onion and garlic. Pour off fat. Add remaining ingredients. Simmer gently about 15 minutes. Add cooked, drained macaroni. Simmer 5 minutes. Remove bay leaf before serving.

*See page 2

Fiesta Beef-Macaroni Casserole

Makes 8 servings   Calories: 260 per serving

2 cups uncooked macaroni
1 pound lean ground beef
¾ cup chopped onion
¼ cup chopped green pepper
1 garlic clove, minced
2 cans (6 ounces each) unsalted tomato paste
2 cups water

½ teaspoon sugar
⅛ teaspoon thyme
1 teaspoon basil
½ teaspoon oregano
¼ teaspoon pepper
2 cups (1 pound) unsalted dry cottage cheese

Cook macaroni as directed on package, omitting salt. Drain and set aside. Place ground beef, onion, green pepper and garlic in large skillet. Cook until meat browns and vegetables are tender. Pour off fat. Add remaining ingredients except for cottage cheese. Cover and simmer gently 5 minutes. Place a thin layer of meat sauce in bottom of a 2-quart casserole. Top with half of the cooked, drained macaroni. Spread cottage cheese over macaroni. Top cottage cheese with half of remaining meat sauce. Cover sauce with remaining macaroni. Pour last of meat sauce over all. Bake in 350°F. oven 45 minutes or until sauce is bubbly and top begins to brown.

Veal à l'Orange

Makes 4 servings   Calories: 205 per serving

4 lean veal chops, cut ½-inch thick, well-trimmed
1 tablespoon oil
½ cup orange juice

1½ teaspoons cornstarch
½ cup water
1 teaspoon sugar
1 orange, peeled and cut into thin slices

Brown chops in oil in large skillet. Pour off fat. Pour orange juice over chops. Cover, reduce heat and cook slowly for 30 minutes. Remove chops and set aside in warm place. Dissolve cornstarch in water and add to orange juice in skillet. Add sugar and orange slices. Cook, stirring constantly until thickened. Return chops to skillet and heat through. May be served over rice.

Veal Curry

Makes 6 servings

Calories: 195 per serving

1½   pounds lean veal shoulder, well trimmed, cut into cubes or slices
3   tablespoons margarine*
½   cup thinly sliced onion

¾   teaspoon curry powder*
3   cups hot water
2   tablespoons cornstarch
½   cup cold water

Place meat and margarine in large skillet and brown. Add onion slices and cook until tender. Pour off fat. Dissolve curry powder in a small amount of hot water. Add this with remaining hot water to meat and onion mixture. Cover and gently simmer 1½ hours or until meat is tender. Combine cornstarch with cold water. Add slowly to curry mixture, stirring constantly until thickened. If a thinner consistency is desired, add more water. May be served over rice to which parsley has been added.

Lemon Veal with Spinach

Makes 6 servings

Calories: 240 per serving

1½   pounds lean veal shoulder, well trimmed, cut into cubes
3   tablespoons oil
1   large onion, chopped
¼   cup water
1   tablespoon lemon juice

¼   teaspoon pepper
½   teaspoon crushed fennel seed
3   green onions, chopped
2   packages (10 ounces each) frozen spinach leaves
1   lemon, cut into 6 wedges

Brown veal in oil in large, heavy skillet. Add chopped onion, cooking until onion is tender. Pour off fat. Add water, lemon juice, pepper and crushed fennel seed. Cover and simmer over low heat 1 hour or until veal is tender, stirring occasionally. More water may be added if needed. Add green onions and spinach. Cover and continue simmering until spinach is tender, about 5-10 minutes. Arrange veal on warm serving platter surrounded with a border of spinach. Garnish with lemon wedges.

*See page 2

27

Pork Sausage Patties

Makes 4 patties

Calories: 125 per patty

- ¾ pound lean ground pork
- ¼ teaspoon pepper
- ¼ teaspoon basil
- ¼ teaspoon sage
- ¼ teaspoon oregano
- ⅛ teaspoon allspice
- ⅛ teaspoon nutmeg
- ⅛ teaspoon dill weed
- ⅛ teaspoon chili powder*, optional
- ⅛ teaspoon hot pepper sauce, optional
- ⅛ teaspoon garlic powder
- 1 egg white
- 2 tablespoons water

Combine all ingredients and mix thoroughly. Shape into 4 patties and place on a rack in a shallow pan. Broil 2-4 inches from the heat 10-15 minutes. Turn patties and broil 5-10 minutes or until well-done.

Hungarian Pork Chops

Makes 4 servings

Calories: 150 per serving

- 4 loin pork chops, very lean, ½ inch-thick, well-trimmed
- 1 teaspoon oil
- 1 teaspoon paprika
- ½ teaspoon caraway seed
- ½ teaspoon dill weed
- ½ teaspoon onion powder
- ½ teaspoon garlic powder
- ½ cup water
- ⅔ cup low-fat plain yogurt, drained as directed on page 17

Brown chops in oil in heavy skillet. Pour off fat. Mix seasonings together and sprinkle over chops. Add water to skillet. Reduce heat, cover tightly and simmer 1 hour or until tender. Add more water if necessary. Remove chops and keep warm. Five minutes before serving, stir drained yogurt into liquid in the pan and mix well. Heat, but do not boil. Serve sauce over chops.

*See page 2

Mediterranean Pork Chops

Makes 4 servings

Calories: 125 per serving

4	loin pork chops, very lean, ½ inch-thick, well-trimmed
1	teaspoon oil
½	teaspoon marjoram

⅛	teaspoon garlic powder
⅛	teaspoon onion powder
⅛	teaspoon pepper
½	cup water

Brown chops in oil in large skillet. Pour off fat. Mix seasonings together and sprinkle over chops. Add water and cover tightly. Reduce heat and simmer over low heat 1 hour or until tender.

Lemon-Barbecued Chicken

Makes 4 servings

Calories: 255 per serving

2½	pound frying chicken, quartered, skinned
dash	paprika
dash	cayenne pepper

¼	cup lemon juice
¼	cup honey
1	tablespoon sesame seeds, toasted

Season chicken lightly with paprika and pepper. Combine lemon juice and honey, mixing thoroughly; set aside 2 tablespoons. Place chicken on broiler rack. Broil 4-5 inches from the heat 15 minutes. Baste occasionally with remaining lemon-honey mixture. Turn pieces over, baste and broil 15 minutes longer or until tender. Combine sesame seeds and reserved lemon-honey mixture. Spoon over chicken just before serving. May be cooked on charcoal grill.

Chicken À L'Orange

Makes 4 servings

Calories: 375 per serving

½ cup all-purpose flour
2 teaspoons freshly-grated orange peel
1 teaspoon paprika
½ teaspoon pepper
2½ pound frying chicken, cut in pieces, skinned

1 tablespoon oil
½ cup water
1½ cups orange juice
2 tablespoons packed brown sugar
¼ teaspoon ginger
⅛ teaspoon cinnamon
¼ cup finely-chopped pecans

Combine flour, orange peel, paprika and pepper. Set aside 2 tablespoons flour mixture and coat chicken with remainder. Brown chicken in oil in large, heavy skillet. More oil may be added if needed. Pour off fat. Add water. Cover and simmer over low heat 30 minutes or until tender. Remove chicken to warm serving platter. Pour off drippings, reserving 2 tablespoons. Return these 2 tablespoons of drippings to skillet. Add reserved seasoned flour mixture. Blend well. Add orange juice, brown sugar, ginger and cinnamon. Cook, stirring constantly until thickened. Serve chicken topped with orange sauce and pecans.

Chicken Italiano

Makes 4 servings

Calories: 350 per serving

3 tablespoons margarine*, melted
1 tablespoon oil
1 teaspoon oregano
¼ teaspoon garlic powder

1 teaspoon paprika
¾ cup dry bread crumbs*
2½ pound frying chicken, cut in pieces, skinned

Combine melted margarine and oil in a shallow baking dish. In separate flat dish, mix together oregano, garlic powder, paprika and bread crumbs. Dip chicken pieces in margarine-oil mixture, then roll each piece in seasoned crumbs, coating evenly. Place in shallow baking dish. Bake uncovered in 350°F. oven 1 hour.

*See page 2

Lemon-Baked Chicken

Makes 4 servings   Calories: 302 per serving

2½   pound frying chicken, cut in
      pieces, skinned
¼   cup oil
¼   cup lemon juice
2   teaspoons oregano or tarragon,
      optional

⅛   teaspoon garlic powder
2   tablespoons chopped parsley
¼   teaspoon paprika

Place chicken pieces in casserole dish. Combine oil, lemon juice, oregano or tarragon and garlic powder and brush on chicken. Cover and bake in 350°F. oven 35 minutes. Remove cover. Brush again with oil-lemon mixture. Continue baking, uncovered, 20 minutes longer or until tender. Sprinkle with parsley and paprika before serving.

Bread Dressing

Makes 4 servings   Calories: 220 per serving

⅓   cup chopped celery
1   small onion, chopped
1   small garlic clove
¼   cup oil
2   medium tart apples, peeled and
      coarsely-grated

2   cups (approximately 3 slices)
      day-old bread*, cut in cubes
¼   teaspoon nutmeg
⅛   teaspoon pepper
1   tablespoon brown sugar

Brown celery, onion and garlic in 1 tablespoon oil. Remove garlic. Add remaining oil, apples, bread, nutmeg, pepper and brown sugar. Mix together lightly. Place dressing in lightly oiled 5 x 7-inch loaf pan. Cover and bake in 350°F. oven 25 minutes. When doubled, this recipe is sufficient to accompany an 8-10 pound turkey.

*See page 2

31

Cacciatore

Calories: 235 per serving

¼ cup oil
1 garlic clove, minced
3 chicken breasts, cut in halves, skinned
1 medium onion, chopped
2 tablespoons chopped green pepper
4 fresh tomatoes, peeled and chopped
¼ cup dry white table wine
¼ teaspoon rosemary
1 bay leaf
¼ teaspoon basil
⅛ teaspoon pepper

Heat oil and garlic in large skillet. Add chicken and brown. Remove chicken. Add onion and green pepper to skillet, adding more oil if necessary. Cook until tender. Pour off fat. Return chicken to skillet. Add remaining ingredients. Cover and simmer over low heat 30 minutes, or until chicken is tender. Remove bay leaf before serving. May be served over rice.

Golden Baked Chicken

Makes 4 servings

Calories: 280 per serving

2½ pound frying chicken, cut in pieces, skinned
¼ cup margarine*, melted
2 tablespoons lemon juice
½ teaspoon paprika
⅛ teaspoon pepper
⅛ teaspoon garlic powder

Place chicken on a rack in a shallow baking dish. Combine remaining ingredients and brush on chicken. Bake in 375°F. oven 1 hour. Brush chicken with margarine mixture once or twice during baking.

*See page 2

Poached Salmon Steaks

Makes 4 servings

Calories: 185 per serving

1	pound salmon steaks*		1	bay leaf
¾	cup water		¼	teaspoon pepper
¾	cup dry white table wine		⅛	teaspoon cloves
1	medium onion, chopped		⅛	teaspoon thyme

Place salmon in a large skillet. Add remaining ingredients. If necessary, add additional water so fish is barely covered with liquid. Simmer over low heat 15-20 minutes or until salmon is firm and flakes easily with a fork. Drain liquid and serve fish with Swedish Dill Sauce, page 87.

Tomato Crown Fish

Makes 6 servings

Calories: 155 per serving

1½	cups water		½	medium green pepper, finely chopped
2	tablespoons lemon juice		2	tablespoons finely chopped onion
1½	pounds cod fillets*		¼	cup dry bread crumbs*
⅛	teaspoon pepper		½	teaspoon basil
2	large fresh tomatoes, sliced ¼ inch thick		1	tablespoon oil

Combine water and lemon juice. Pour over fish fillets and let stand 30 minutes. Drain fillets. Place fish in an oiled baking dish. Season with pepper. Place tomato slices on fish and sprinkle with green pepper and onion. Combine bread crumbs, basil and oil, blending well. Spread seasoned crumb mixture evenly over tomatoes. Bake uncovered in 350°F. oven 25 minutes or until fish is firm and flakes easily with a fork.

*See page 2

Rolled Fish Fillets

Makes 8 servings

Calories: 115 per serving

2 pounds fish fillets*
3 tablespoons lemon juice

1½ cups water or more
1 bay leaf

Dip fish fillets in lemon juice. Drain. Beginning with the narrow end, roll each fillet as for jelly roll and secure with a toothpick. Place water in saucepan. Water should be 2 inches deep. Add bay leaf and bring to a boil. Carefully place rolled fillets in boiling water, cover and reduce heat. Simmer 5 minutes or until fish is firm and flakes easily with a fork. Carefully transfer fillets to a heated serving platter. Remove toothpicks. Serve with Lemon Parsley Sauce, page 86, or chopped toasted almonds.

Tuna-Macaroni Casserole

Makes 4 servings

Calories: 305 per serving

1 cup uncooked macaroni
1 tablespoon oil
2 tablespoons chopped onion
1 tablespoon all-purpose flour
¼ teaspoon curry powder*
¼ teaspoon onion powder
⅛ teaspoon pepper
1 tablespoon finely chopped parsley
    Bell Pepper

or ½ tablespoon dry parsley flakes
1 cup skim milk
½ cup drained canned tomatoes*, chopped
1 can (6½ ounces) unsalted tuna, drained
2 tablespoons margarine*, melted
¼ cup dry bread crumbs*

Cook macaroni as directed on package, omitting salt. Drain and set aside. Heat oil in saucepan. Add chopped onion and cook until tender. Add flour, curry and onion powders, pepper and parsley. Mix thoroughly. Gradually stir in milk, blending well. Cook, stirring constantly, until mixture comes to a boil. Remove from heat. Add macaroni, tomatoes and tuna. Pour into lightly-oiled 1½-quart casserole. In separate pan, combine melted margarine and bread crumbs. Sprinkle evenly over top of tuna-macaroni mixture. Bake in 350°F. oven 30-35 minutes or until sauce is bubbly.

*See page 2

Herbed Fillet of Sole

Makes 4 servings

Calories: 165 per serving

⅓   cup lemon juice
¼   teaspoon dry mustard powder
½   teaspoon tarragon

2   tablespoons margarine*
1   pound fillet of sole*

Combine lemon juice, mustard and tarragon. Spread margarine in flat baking dish and add fish. Brush with seasoned lemon juice. Broil 2-3 inches from the heat 5-8 minutes for thin fillets (10-12 minutes for thicker fillets). Brush once or twice with lemon juice mixture during broiling. Fish is done when it is firm and flakes easily with a fork. Do not overcook.

Tuna Oriental

Makes 3 servings

Calories: 185 per serving

½   green pepper, cut in ¼-inch strips
1   small onion, thinly sliced
2   teaspoons oil
⅓   cup pineapple juice
1½   teaspoons cornstarch
⅔   cup drained pineapple chunks
     (canned in juice)

1   tablespoon sugar
1   tablespoon vinegar
1   can (6½ ounces) unsalted tuna,
     drained and flaked
⅛   teaspoon pepper
dash hot pepper sauce

Cook green pepper and onion in oil, leaving slightly crisp. Mix pineapple juice with cornstarch and add to green pepper and onion mixture. Cook, stirring gently until thickened. Add remaining ingredients. Cook 5 minutes, stirring occasionally. May be served over rice.

*See page 2

Oven-Fried Fish

Makes 4 servings

Calories: 300 per serving

¼ cup margarine*, melted
1 tablespoon lemon juice
¼ teaspoon pepper
¼ teaspoon paprika
¼ teaspoon basil

⅛ teaspoon garlic powder
1 pound fillet of flounder* or other fish
¼ cup dry bread crumbs*
2 tablespoons oil

Combine margarine, lemon juice, pepper, paprika, basil and garlic. Dredge fish in margarine-herb mixture and roll in bread crumbs. Spread oil in shallow baking dish and arrange fish in one layer. Spoon remaining margarine mixture over fish. Bake uncovered in 475°F. oven 15 minutes or until fish flakes easily with a fork.

Lamb Curry

Makes 8 servings

Calories: 155 per serving

3 tablespoons all-purpose flour
⅛ teaspoon pepper
2 pounds lean lamb, well trimmed, cut into cubes
2 tablespoons oil

½ cup finely chopped onion
2 teaspoons curry powder*
3 cups water
2 teaspoons lemon juice

Combine flour and pepper. Roll lamb in seasoned flour; brown in oil in large skillet. Pour off fat. Add onion, curry powder and water. Cover and simmer over low heat, stirring occasionally for 1 hour or until meat is tender. Stir in lemon juice. May be served over rice and garnished with unsalted peanuts.

*See page 2

36

No-Cholesterol Egg Substitute

Makes ½ cup

Calories: 200 per recipe

4 egg whites
1 tablespoon oil

1 tablespoon non-fat dry milk powder
3 drops yellow food coloring

Combine all ingredients. Mix until well-blended. Use in place of 2 whole eggs in your recipes. This substitution may require some experimenting in baking since it will not work in every cake and cookie recipe.

Variations: **No-Cholesterol Scrambled Eggs** — Add a dash of thyme and a dash of pepper. Melt a small amount of margarine* in a small skillet. Cook over low heat, stirring occasionally, until dry.

No-Cholesterol Omelet — Place a small amount of margarine* in a small saucepan. Melt over moderate heat. Add egg substitute and cook until lightly browned. Turn omelet and brown other side. Place chopped fresh tomatoes or sauteed sliced mushrooms, onions, green pepper, or chives in center of omelet and fold in half.

French Toast

Makes 5 servings

Calories: 150 per serving

1 recipe No-Cholesterol Egg Substitute, page 37
¼ cup skim milk
¼ teaspoon vanilla

⅛ teaspoon cinnamon
5 slices day-old bread*
2 tablespoons margarine*

Mix egg substitute, skim milk, vanilla and cinnamon. Dip bread slices in egg mixture. Melt margarine in skillet and lightly brown bread slices. May be served with margarine and syrup or jelly.

*See page 2

Baked Beans

Makes 6 servings

Calories: 180 per serving

½ pound (1 cup) dried navy beans
4 cups water
1 loin end pork chop, very lean, well-trimmed
1 cup unsalted chili sauce

¾ cup chopped onion
2 tablespoons molasses
1 tablespoon packed brown sugar
1½ teaspoons dry mustard powder
¼ teaspoon garlic powder

Place beans and water in a saucepan. Bring to a boil and cook 2 minutes. Set aside for one hour. Return to heat and simmer 1 hour or until beans are tender. Drain beans, reserving the cooking water. Place beans in an oiled 1½-quart casserole. Set aside. Brown pork chop in a small skillet.

Cut into small cubes and add to beans. Add remaining ingredients plus one cup of reserved cooking water. Mix well. Cover casserole and bake in 350°F. oven 4 hours. If needed, add additional reserved cooking water.

Cheese Blintzes

Makes 22 blintzes

Calories: 80 per blintz

1 recipe Crepes, page 78
2 cups (1 pound) unsalted dry cottage cheese
1 egg white

¼ cup sugar
½ teaspoon grated fresh lemon peel
2 tablespoons fresh lemon juice

Prepare crepes. To make filling, combine all ingredients and beat well. Place 1 tablespoon of filling in center of each crepe and fold in an envelope shape. Blintzes may be refrigerated for up to 5 hours. When ready to serve, heat blintzes

in approximately 1 tablespoon of margarine* 10 minutes or until heated through. May be topped with a sprinkle of cinnamon and sugar or with warm applesauce and cinnamon.

*See page 2

Tacos

Makes 4 servings

Calories: 315 per serving

1 pound lean ground beef
1 can (1 pound) unsalted tomato puree
½ teaspoon chili powder*
¼ teaspoon garlic powder
¼ teaspoon onion powder
¼ teaspoon sugar
¼ teaspoon pepper
2 cups oil, approximately
12 frozen tortillas, thawed
½ cup chopped green pepper
½ cup chopped onion
2 fresh tomatoes, chopped
½ head lettuce, shredded

Brown meat in large skillet. Pour off fat. Add tomato puree, chili, garlic and onion powders, sugar and black pepper. Mix well. Cook uncovered over low heat 1 hour or until thick. Stir occasionally. Using a fat thermometer as a guide, heat oil to 375°F. in a deep saucepan (oil must be 3 inches deep). Fry tortillas in oil until crisp, holding them in an envelope position with 2 spatulas. Drain on paper towels. To serve, spoon meat mixture into tortillas and top with green pepper, onion, tomato and lettuce. Leftover tortillas may be broken into chip-sized pieces and eaten as a snack. The oil may be strained, refrigerated and reused.

Sloppy Joes

Makes 8 servings

Calories: 240 per serving

1½ pounds lean ground beef
½ cup finely-chopped onion
1 tablespoon packed brown sugar
1 tablespoon vinegar
1 teaspoon dry mustard powder
2 tablespoons water
½ cup unsalted catsup
8 hamburger buns*

Brown ground beef and onion together. Pour off fat. Add brown sugar, vinegar, mustard powder, water and catsup. Simmer over low heat 5 minutes or until warm. Serve over hamburger buns which have been split open and toasted.

*See page 2

Spaghetti with Mushroom Sauce

Makes 6 servings

Calories: 225 per serving

3 tablespoons margarine*
1 cup sliced fresh mushrooms
⅓ cup chopped onion
1 garlic clove, minced
1 can (1 pound) tomatoes*
1 can (6 ounces) unsalted tomato paste
½ cup water

1 tablespoon sugar
1 bay leaf
¼ teaspoon basil
¼ teaspoon oregano
⅛ teaspoon pepper
1 package (8 ounces) dry spaghetti, cooked without salt

Melt margarine in large skillet. Add mushrooms, onion and garlic. Cook until onion is tender. Stir in remaining ingredients except for spaghetti. Cover and simmer over low heat 2 hours, stirring occasionally. If sauce appears too thick, add additional water. Remove bay leaf. Serve over spaghetti.

Spaghetti with Meat Sauce

Makes 6 servings

Calories: 270 per serving

1 pound lean ground beef
1 medium onion, chopped
1 garlic clove, minced
5 medium fresh tomatoes, peeled and chopped, or 1 large can (28 ounces) tomatoes*, chopped
1 can (6 ounces) unsalted tomato paste

½ cup dry red table wine
½ teaspoon oregano
½ teaspoon basil
½ teaspoon fennel seed
⅛ teaspoon pepper
1 package (8 ounces) dry spaghetti, cooked without salt

Brown ground beef in a large skillet. Pour off fat. Add remaining ingredients except for spaghetti. Cover and simmer over low heat 1½ hours, stirring occasionally. If sauce appears too thick, add water. Serve over spaghetti.

*See page 2

Fried Rice

Makes 6 servings

Calories: 210 per serving

¼ cup oil
3 tablespoons chopped onion
3 tablespoons chopped celery
¼ cup chopped green pepper
½ cup sliced fresh mushrooms
1½ cups uncooked instant rice or
1 cup uncooked raw rice

½ cup unsalted, cooked and
    diced chicken or turkey
¼ teaspoon curry powder*
¼ teaspoon paprika

Heat oil in skillet. Add onion, celery, green pepper and mushrooms. Cook until onion is tender. Follow package directions for rice, omitting salt. Add rice and continue to cook until rice is slightly browned. Add remaining ingredients. Mix and heat through.

Seasoned Rice

Makes 4 servings

Calories: 280 per serving

⅓ cup margarine*
1 medium onion, finely chopped
¾ cup uncooked long-grain rice
2 unsalted chicken bouillon cubes
1½ cups boiling water

¼ teaspoon celery flakes
¼ teaspoon onion powder
¼ teaspoon dill weed
⅛ teaspoon pepper

Melt margarine in skillet. Add onion and rice. Brown lightly. Dissolve bouillon cubes in boiling water. Add to rice-onion mixture. Add remaining ingredients and bring to a boil. Cover, reduce heat and simmer 15-25 minutes or until rice is tender.

*See page 2

Sandwiches

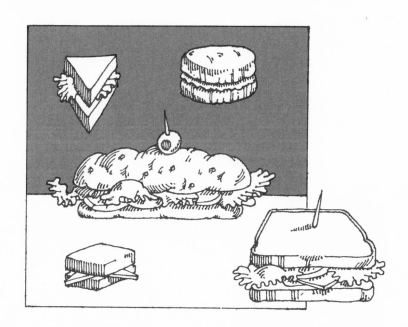

Sandwiches

The sandwich is a flexible addition to any cook's repertoire. They're great for lunchboxes, can be cut into fancy shapes for canapés and are quick and easy meals to make at home when accompanied by soup or salad and a dessert. However, if you are following a sodium-modified and fat-modified diet, there are some types of sandwiches you should avoid — those made with cold cuts, corned beef, hot dogs, cheese and eggs.

With advance planning, you can make and enjoy a variety of sandwiches. Begin by preparing more meat than you need for a single meal. Slice or divide the leftover meat into individual servings and then either freeze the servings separately or make the meat into sandwiches and then freeze them. To ensure freshness, place each individual sandwich in a plastic bag and then wrap it in heavy foil before freezing. It's also a good idea to mark the date on the package. Frozen sandwiches will usually retain their flavor for about one month. When placed in a lunchbox in the morning, the sandwiches will be thawed and just as tasty by lunchtime as those that have been prepared on the same day.

Almost all meat sandwiches can be frozen. Pack such extras as lettuce, tomatoes and mayonnaise in a separate container and add them to your sandwich when you are ready to eat. To add variety to your sandwiches, try some of the following suggestions:

Breads:
Use different types of bread such as: bagels, hard rolls, English muffins, Italian, pumpernickel, rye, Vienna or whole wheat.

Spreads:
Use plain margarine or margarine seasoned with: dry mustard powder, grated lemon or orange rind, minced green pepper, chives, onion juice or minced onion. Mayonnaise, mustard or unsalted catsup or unsalted chili sauce may also be used.

Fillings:
Thin slices of beef with: onion and freshly ground black pepper, thin slices of cucumber or tomato with mustard, grated fresh horseradish.

Thin slices of lamb, veal or chicken with: mint, currant or cranberry jelly.

Thin slices of pork with: chopped raisins or prunes combined with unsalted French dressing, apple butter or applesauce.

Ground or chopped leftover meats mixed with: mayonnaise, unsalted chili sauce and chopped onion.

Peanut butter with: jelly or honey, thin slices of green pepper or cucumber, apple or banana slices, unsalted pickles.

Chicken-Pineapple Salad

Makes 6 servings   Calories: 175 per serving

2 cups unsalted, cooked and diced chicken
1 can (8 ounces) crushed pineapple, drained
2 tablespoons finely-chopped green pepper
¼ cup mayonnaise*

Mix all ingredients together. Chill. Serve on bread as a sandwich or on lettuce leaves for a main dish salad.

Chicken Salad

Makes 6 servings   Calories: 215 per serving

2 cups unsalted, cooked and diced chicken
½ cup chopped celery
⅛ teaspoon dry mustard powder
1 teaspoon lemon juice
½ cup mayonnaise*

Toss chicken with celery. Combine dry mustard, lemon juice and mayonnaise and mix well. Pour over chicken mixture and stir until well-mixed. Chill. Use as a sandwich filling or serve on lettuce leaves for a main dish salad. May be garnished with any of the following: grapes, cut in half and seeded; pineapple chunks; fresh tomato wedges; toasted, unsalted almonds or pecans.

Variation: **Turkey Salad** – Use turkey in place of chicken.

*See page 2

Tuna Salad

Makes 3 servings   Calories: 180 per serving

1 can (6½ ounces) unsalted tuna, drained
½ cup chopped, unpeeled cucumber

3 tablespoons mayonnaise*
⅛ teaspoon onion powder
⅛ teaspoon dry mustard powder

Toss flaked tuna with cucumber. Combine mayonnaise, onion powder and mustard and mix well. Pour over tuna mixture and stir until well-mixed. Chill. Use as a sandwich filling or serve on lettuce leaves for a main dish salad.

Mock Cream Cheese

Makes 1¼ cups   Calories: 120 per ¼ cup

1 cup (8 ounces) unsalted dry cottage cheese

¼ cup margarine*, softened
skim milk, if needed

Mix margarine and cottage cheese thoroughly in blender. If mixture appears too thick to spread, add skim milk, 1 teaspoon at a time, until the desired consistency is reached. Cover tightly and store in refrigerator. Use as a sandwich spread topped with marmalade, jam or honey.

Deviled Beef Spread

Makes 2 servings   Calories: 165 per serving

1 cup finely-chopped, cooked, lean rump or round roast of beef
2 tablespoons chopped celery
3 tablespoons unsalted chili sauce

2 teaspoons mayonnaise*
¼ teaspoon dry mustard powder
⅛ teaspoon pepper

Toss beef with celery and chili sauce. Combine remaining ingredients and mix well. Pour over beef mixture and stir until well-blended. Chill. Use as a sandwich filling. Variation: **Deviled Veal Spread** — Use cooked veal in place of beef.

*See page 2

46

Vegetables

Vegetables

When cooking vegetables, there are many flavorings you can add in place of salt. For example, peas, carrots and corn are more tasty when cooked with margarine and a dash of sugar. The flavor of beans, corn or asparagus is enhanced by adding a dash or two of hot pepper sauce or a sprinkle of crushed red pepper.

Foods such as bacon and salt pork should not be used to flavor vegetables as they add large amounts of sodium and saturated fat. Try unsalted liquid smoke or some of the following suggestions for new taste adventures.

Vegetables can be flavored by using Herbed Margarine, page 88, a bit of lemon juice or peel, a pinch of dill or a touch of thyme. Toppings such as fresh mushrooms, pimiento, onions, unsalted almonds or water chestnuts can add color, crunch and flavor.

You can also make your own "saucy" vegetables with Swedish Dill Sauce, page 87, Mushroom Sauce, page 88 and Vinaigrette Dressing, Page 66. A mixture of different vegetables with pineapple, orange or cranberry juice added will have a Polynesian flavor.

You can experiment with a cooking technique known as stir frying. Cut vegetables in thin strips, place a small amount of oil in a pan and, stirring constantly, fry vegetables quickly until tender but still crisp. You'll discover they will taste almost like fresh vegetables. Again, herbs and spices may be added for flavor. Don't be afraid to try unfamiliar herbs and spices. Start with a small amount and taste test as you add more. For some helpful hints on seasoning, see page 13.

Potatoes boiled or baked in their skins are much more flavorful than those peeled before cooking. Mock Sour Cream, page 84, or melted margarine with a few drops of hot pepper sauce adds a zip to baked potatoes. Chopped chives or green onion and a sprinkle of paprika on potatoes is delicious and attractive, too.

Gingered Carrots

Makes 5 servings

Calories: 105 per serving

1   pound raw carrots, peeled and cut into ¼-inch slices
¼   teaspoon ginger
1   teaspoon sugar

¼   cup margarine*, melted
2   tablespoons finely-chopped parsley or 1 tablespoon dry parsley flakes

Place carrots in saucepan. Add just enough water to cover. Boil 10-12 minutes or until barely tender. Drain. Mix ginger with sugar; sprinkle over carrots; add melted margarine and stir gently. Sprinkle with parsley just before serving.

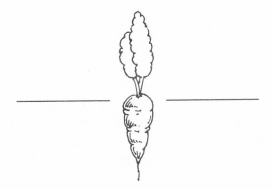

Fried Cabbage with Noodles

Makes 6 servings

Calories: 130 per serving

1   cup dry noodles
3   cups finely-chopped cabbage
2   tablespoons margarine*

¾   teaspoon caraway seeds
½   teaspoon onion powder

Cook noodles according to package directions, omitting salt. Stir-fry chopped cabbage in margarine over medium heat until cabbage is tender but still crisp, about 5-8 minutes. Add drained noodles, caraway seeds and onion powder. Stir together gently.

*See page 2

Broccoli Western Style

Makes 3 servings

Calories: 185 per serving

2 tablespoons lemon juice
¼ teaspoon pepper
¼ teaspoon oregano
¼ garlic clove

¼ cup oil
1 package (10 ounces) frozen or 1 pound fresh broccoli

Mix all ingredients together except broccoli. Let stand 30 minutes. Cook frozen broccoli according to directions on package, omitting salt. If using fresh broccoli, wash, trim, cut into small stalks and cook in boiling unsalted water 10-15 minutes or until tender but still crisp. Remove garlic from dressing, stir well and pour over hot broccoli just before serving. Variation: **Green Beans Western Style** — Use green beans in place of broccoli.

Sauteed Cauliflower

Makes 4 servings

Calories: 75 per serving

1 head (1 pound) fresh or 1 package (10 ounces) frozen cauliflower
2 tablespoons oil
¼ teaspoon thyme
¾ teaspoon vinegar

½ garlic clove, minced
dash pepper
2 teaspoons minced parsley or 1 teaspoon dry parsley flakes

Break cauliflower into small flowerettes and cook or steam in unsalted water until just tender, 10-12 minutes; or cook frozen cauliflower according to directions on package, omitting salt. Drain. Combine and heat oil, thyme, vinegar and garlic in a large pan or skillet over moderate heat 5 minutes. Add drained cauliflower, sprinkle with pepper and stir gently. Simmer until hot. Sprinkle with parsley just before serving.

Eggplant Mexicana

Makes 6 servings

Calories: 30 per serving

1 medium (1 pound) eggplant, peeled and cut into cubes
1 can (16 ounces) tomatoes* or 4 medium fresh tomatoes, peeled and chopped

1 garlic clove, minced
2 tablespoons chopped onion
¼ teaspoon chili powder*
dash pepper

Combine all ingredients in skillet and simmer gently 15-20 minutes or until eggplant is tender.

Boiled Greens

Makes 4 servings

Calories: 145 per serving

1-1½ pounds beef shank or neck bones
4 cups water
¼ teaspoon dried red pepper flakes
1 package (10 ounces) frozen turnip greens or 2 pounds fresh collard or turnip greens
¼ cup oil
1 tablespoon sugar
2 tablespoons vinegar

Combine bones, water and pepper flakes in a saucepan. Bring to a boil, reduce heat, cover and simmer 4 hours. Remove bones, strain broth and chill. Remove hardened fat from top and discard. Boil broth uncovered until volume is reduced to about 1 cup. Add frozen greens and cook 30 minutes; or add washed, fresh greens and cook over medium heat 45 minutes. Stir in oil, sugar and vinegar just before serving.

*See page 2

Sweet and Sour Green Beans

Makes 4 servings

Calories: 40 per serving

1 package (10 ounces) frozen or 1 pound fresh green beans, cut in 1-inch pieces
1 teaspoon margarine*
½ teaspoon all-purpose flour

1 tablespoon water
1 tablespoon lemon juice
1 tablespoon sugar
¼ teaspoon dill seeds, optional
dash paprika

Cook frozen green beans according to directions on package, omitting salt, or cook fresh green beans in ½ cup unsalted water until tender. Drain and set aside. In separate pan, melt margarine, stir in flour and brown lightly. Stir in remaining ingredients and cook over low heat until thickened. Pour over drained green beans and heat 5 minutes.

Green Beans and Corn

Makes 4 servings

Calories: 70 per serving

1 cup fresh or frozen French-style green beans
1 cup frozen whole kernel corn or fresh, cut from cob
½ cup water

1 tablespoon margarine*
3 tablespoons chopped onion
½ teaspoon lemon juice
dash pepper
½ teaspoon basil

Cook beans and corn together in water until beans are just tender. Drain. In a separate pan, cook onion in margarine until tender. Pour over beans and corn and add basil, lemon juice and pepper. Simmer until hot.

Variation: **Succotash** — Use fresh lima beans in place of green beans.

*See page 2

Sauteed Mushrooms on Toast

Makes 4 servings

Calories: 180 per serving

1   medium onion, finely chopped
3   tablespoons margarine*
1   pound fresh mushrooms, sliced

2   teaspoons lemon juice
dash   pepper
4   slices bread*, toasted

Cook onion in margarine until tender. Add mushrooms, cover and cook over low heat 8-10 minutes or until mushrooms are tender. Sprinkle with lemon juice and pepper. Serve over toast as a meat accompaniment.

Stuffed Green Peppers

Makes 4 servings

Calories: 130 per serving

2   medium green peppers
2   fresh tomatoes, peeled and chopped
¼   cup chopped onion
¼   cup chopped fresh mushrooms

2   tablespoons chopped chives
⅛   teaspoon basil
¼   teaspoon pepper
½   cup bread crumbs*
2   tablespoons margarine*, melted

Cut peppers in half lengthwise, remove tops and seeds. Cover with water and parboil 5 minutes. Remove from water and place cut side up in shallow baking dish. Combine remaining ingredients, except bread crumbs and margarine, and mix well. Fill each pepper half with mixture. Mix bread crumbs with melted margarine and sprinkle over filled peppers. Pour ¼ inch of water into bottom of dish and bake in 350°F. oven 25-30 minutes.

*See page 2

Scalloped Potatoes

Makes 5 servings

Calories: 195 per serving

3 tablespoons margarine*
2 tablespoons all-purpose flour
2 cups skim milk
¼ teaspoon pepper

⅛ teaspoon onion powder
⅛ teaspoon garlic powder
5 medium potatoes, thinly sliced
½ cup chopped onion

Melt margarine in a small saucepan. Add flour and mix well. Gradually add milk while stirring constantly. Cook over medium heat, stirring until thickened. Add pepper, onion powder and garlic powder. Place potatoes and chopped onion in a lightly-oiled 1 ½-quart casserole, add sauce and mix. Cover and bake in 350°F. oven 30 minutes. Stir gently and bake uncovered an additional 30-40 minutes or until lightly browned and potatoes are tender.

Potatoes O'Brien

Makes 5 servings

Calories: 145 per serving

5 medium potatoes, unpeeled
2 medium onions, chopped
1 small green pepper, chopped

2 tablespoons oil
⅛ teaspoon pepper
⅛ teaspoon paprika

Boil potatoes in water 20-25 minutes until tender. Peel and cut into 1-inch cubes. In a large skillet, cook onions and green pepper in oil until tender. Add potatoes and sprinkle with pepper and paprika. Cook over medium heat 10 minutes or until potatoes are browned, stirring frequently.

*See page 2

54

Hash-Browned Potatoes

Makes 6 servings

Calories: 245 per serving

½   cup oil
¼   teaspoon pepper
⅛   teaspoon onion powder
⅛   teaspoon garlic powder

6   cups chopped or grated raw
      potatoes
dash paprika

Combine oil, pepper and onion and garlic powders in a large skillet. Heat. Add potatoes. Fry until crisp, stirring frequently. Add paprika while frying. Drain on paper towels.

Dilled Summer Squash

Makes 4 servings

Calories: 40 per serving

2   medium summer squash, sliced
¼   cup water
1½   teaspoons finely chopped onion

½   teaspoon dill seed, crushed
⅛   teaspoon pepper
1   tablespoon margarine*

Cook squash in water with onion, dill seed and pepper 10 minutes or until tender. Drain and dot with margarine.

Baked Tomatoes

Makes 4 servings

Calories: 45 per serving

2   tomatoes, cut in halves
1   tablespoon oil
½   teaspoon chopped parsley or

¼   teaspoon dry parsley flakes
¼   teaspoon oregano
¼   teaspoon basil

Place tomato halves in a lightly-oiled baking dish. Drizzle oil over tomatoes and
See page 2
sprinkle with remaining ingredients. Bake in 350°F. oven 20-30 minutes.

Sweet Potato Casserole

Makes 6 servings

Calories: 150 per serving

4 medium sweet potatoes
1 tablespoon margarine*
¼ cup orange juice

2 tablespoons chopped walnuts
¼ teaspoon nutmeg

Cook whole sweet potatoes in boiling water 25-30 minutes or until tender. Peel and mash. Add remaining ingredients. Mix thoroughly. Place in a lightly-oiled 1-quart casserole. Bake uncovered in 375°F. oven 25 minutes.

Scalloped Sweet Potatoes

Makes 6 servings

Calories: 185 per serving

¼ cup sugar
½ teaspoon cinnamon
3 raw, medium sweet potatoes, peeled, sliced ¼-inch thick

2 medium apples, sliced
3 tablespoons margarine*

Mix sugar and cinnamon together. Place a layer of sweet potatoes in a lightly-oiled 1 ½-quart casserole. Add a layer of apples, sprinkle with cinnamon-sugar mixture and dot with margarine. Repeat layers. Cover and bake in 350°F. oven 1 hour.

*See page 2

Potato Pancakes

Makes 8 pancakes

Calories: 95 per pancake

1¼ cups grated raw potatoes
2 tablespoons finely-chopped onion
2 egg whites
¼ cup all-purpose flour
¾ teaspoon baking powder*

¼ teaspoon onion powder
¼ teaspoon garlic powder
⅛ teaspoon pepper
¼ cup oil, approximately

Mix together potatoes and onion. Beat egg whites until they form soft peaks and fold into the potato mixture. Add remaining ingredients except oil and mix well. Heat oil in large skillet. Spoon batter into skillet and spread to ½-inch thickness. When browned, turn and cook second side. Drain on paper towels. May be served with warm applesauce sprinkled with cinnamon.

Stuffed Mushrooms

Makes 4 servings

Calories: 140 per serving

16 medium, fresh mushrooms
1 small onion, chopped
3 tablespoons margarine*
1 slice bread*, torn into small pieces
½ cup unsalted, cooked and chopped chicken

2 tablespoons table sherry
¼ teaspoon marjoram
⅛ teaspoon pepper
⅛ teaspoon oregano

Remove and chop stems of mushrooms. Cook onion and mushroom stems in 1 tablespoon margarine until tender. Add all ingredients except remaining margarine. Place mushroom caps, round side up, on baking sheet. Melt remaining margarine and brush mushroom caps with half of it. Broil 2 minutes. Invert caps and fill with chicken mixture. Brush with remaining melted margarine. Broil 3 minutes or until mushrooms are tender and lightly browned on top. Serve as a meat accompaniment, appetizer or canapé.

*See page 2

Salads and Salad Dressings

Salads and Salad Dressings

You can serve salads in many exciting and attractive ways. A salad can be used as a side dish by combining fresh or cooked vegetables or a mixture of fruits. It can even be a meal in itself when topped with meat, poultry, unsalted tuna or salmon or unsalted dry cottage cheese.

Stuffed tomatoes are always a decorative and tasty dish. Scoop out the inside of a ripe tomato and stuff it with a mixture of the remaining pulp plus chopped raw vegetables, mayonnaise and chilled, chopped meat. You may also substitute poultry, unsalted tuna or unsalted salmon for the chopped meat. Tomatoes can also be filled with potato or macaroni salad or sliced cucumbers which have been marinated in oil, vinegar and sugar.

You can give zip to potato salad by adding a little extra white or wine vinegar and a dash of dry mustard or curry powder. Coleslaw makes a taste-tempting salad when combined with fruits such as pineapple, apples, pears or peaches.

Since most commercial salad dressings contain a lot of salt, you should look for dressings made without salt in the special diet section of your grocery store. You may wish to prepare your own, using recipes in this section or your own favorite recipes, omitting salt and salty ingredients. Instead of salt, use herbs and spices such as basil, chervil, coriander, mint, parsley, pepper and tarragon for flavoring.

Marinating is another delicious way to prepare fruit or vegetable salads. Lemon juice, vinegar, vinegar and oil or even a lemon-honey mixture can be tasty toppings for salad dishes.

You can expand your creativity even further by combining fruit or fresh vegetables with flavored or unflavored gelatin and serving the salad on a bed of crisp lettuce.

Pineapple Coleslaw

Makes 5 servings

Calories: 150 per serving

2	cups shredded cabbage
¼	cup chopped green pepper
1	can (15 ¼ ounces) crushed pineapple, drained

¼	cup mayonnaise*
1½	teaspoons vinegar
¼	teaspoon dill weed
⅛	teaspoon pepper

Combine cabbage, green pepper and crushed pineapple. Toss lightly. In a separate bowl, combine remaining ingredients. Mix well. Add to cabbage mixture and blend thoroughly. Chill well before serving.

Waldorf Salad

Makes 6 servings

Calories: 210 per serving

4	medium apples, unpeeled, cored and diced
¼	cup chopped walnuts
¼	cup chopped celery

| ½ | cup grapes, cut in halves and seeded |
| ½ | cup mayonnaise* |

Combine all ingredients and mix well. Chill thoroughly before serving.

Ambrosia

Makes 6 servings

Calories: 125 per serving

¼	recipe or ½ cup Mock Sour Cream, page 84
¼	cup powdered sugar
¼	teaspoon vanilla
1	can (15 ounces) pineapple chunks, drained

1	can (11 ounces) mandarin orange segments, drained
½	cup miniature marshmallows
6	lettuce leaves

Mix mock sour cream, powdered sugar and vanilla. Add fruit and marshmallows and toss together lightly. Chill for at least 1 hour. Serve on salad plates lined with lettuce leaves.

*See page 2

61

Three Bean Salad

Makes 14 servings

Calories: 185 per serving

¾ cup dried kidney beans
4 cups water
1 package (10 ounces) frozen or 1 pound fresh cut green beans
1 package (10 ounces) frozen or 1 pound fresh cut yellow beans
¾ cup vinegar

¾ cup sugar
¾ cup oil
½ teaspoon pepper
1 medium onion, sliced
1 garlic clove
½ green pepper, chopped

Place kidney beans and water in a saucepan. Bring to a boil and cook for 2 minutes. Set aside for 1 hour without draining. Return beans to heat and simmer for 1 hour or until beans are very tender. Drain. Cook green and yellow beans until tender and drain. Heat vinegar and sugar together to dissolve sugar. Add oil, garlic and pepper and mix. Toss vinegar mixture with beans, onion and green pepper. Cover and chill overnight or for 6 hours. Remove garlic clove before serving.
Variation: **Bean and Sprout Salad —** Add 1 cup fresh bean sprouts with cooked beans.

Marinated Tomato Slices

Makes 4 servings

Calories: 85 per serving

3 medium fresh tomatoes, sliced ¼ inch thick
4 lettuce leaves
⅛ teaspoon garlic powder
⅛ teaspoon pepper

¼ teaspoon basil
1 tablespoon dried minced onion
1 tablespoon wine vinegar
2 tablespoons oil

Arrange tomato slices over lettuce on serving platter. In a separate bowl, combine remaining ingredients and mix well. Spoon a small amount of marinade on each tomato slice. Cover and place in refrigerator for one hour. Serve.

Potato Salad

Makes 6 servings   Calories: 220 per serving

5   medium red skin potatoes,
    cooked, peeled and diced
¾   cup chopped celery with leaves
½   cup sliced red radishes
2   green onions, diced
½   cup mayonnaise*
1   teaspoon dry mustard powder

1   tablespoon sugar
¼   teaspoon pepper
¼   teaspoon turmeric
½   teaspoon celery seed, optional
2½   tablespoons white vinegar
3   tablespoons skim milk

Combine potatoes, celery, radishes and
onion. In a separate bowl, mix together
mayonnaise, mustard powder, sugar,
pepper, turmeric and celery seed. Add

vinegar and milk and stir until mixed.
Combine with potato mixture and stir
well. Chill before serving.

Orange-Grapefruit Salad

Makes 3 servings   Calories: 145 per serving

1   large orange, peeled and sectioned
1   large grapefruit, peeled and
    sectioned
1   green onion and top, chopped

1½   tablespoons oil
1½   tablespoons vinegar
3   large lettuce leaves

Combine orange and grapefruit sections
and onion. Chill. When ready to serve,
mix oil and vinegar together with fork

and toss lightly with fruit. Divide fruit
mixture into three portions and serve on
lettuce leaves.

*See page 2

Macaroni Salad

Makes 4 servings   Calories: 220 per serving

1	cup uncooked macaroni	¼	cup chopped cucumber
¼	cup mayonnaise*	¼	cup chopped celery
1	tablespoon sugar	2	radishes, sliced
2	teaspoons vinegar	1	tablespoon finely-chopped onion
⅛	teaspoon pepper		

Cook macaroni according to package directions, omitting salt. Drain and cool. Mix mayonnaise, sugar, vinegar and pepper together to make a dressing. Toss all ingredients together. Chill.

Basic Salad Dressing

Makes 1 cup   Calories: 80 per tablespoon

⅔	cup oil	¼	teaspoon sugar
⅓	cup vinegar	⅛	teaspoon pepper
¼	teaspoon dry mustard powder	⅛	teaspoon garlic powder

Place all ingredients in a jar and shake well. Chill.

Tomato French Dressing

Makes 1¼ cups   Calories: 70 per tablespoon

1	recipe Basic Salad Dressing, page 64	¼	teaspoon dry mustard powder
¼	cup unsalted tomato paste	¼	teaspoon onion powder
2	teaspoons sugar	dash	hot pepper sauce

Place all ingredients in a jar and shake well, Chill.

*See page 2

Italian Dressing

Makes 1¼ cups   Calories: 65 per tablespoon

1   recipe Basic Salad Dressing, page   ¼   teaspoon basil
    64   ⅛   teaspoon garlic powder
3   tablespoons lemon juice   ⅛   teaspoon oregano

Place all ingredients in a jar and shake well. Chill.

Russian Dressing

Makes 1¼ cups   Calories: 65 per tablespoon

1   recipe Basic Salad Dressing, page   ¼   teaspoon chili powder*
    64   ⅛   teaspoon onion powder
2   tablespoons unsalted tomato paste   dash   hot pepper sauce
1   tablespoon finely-chopped green
    pepper

Place all ingredients in a jar and shake well. Chill.

Lemon-Poppy Seed Dressing

Makes 1 cup   Calories: 55 per tablespoon

½   cup frozen lemonade concentrate,   2   tablespoons oil
    undiluted   1   teaspoon poppy seeds
⅓   cup honey

Combine all ingredients in a small mixing   smooth. Serve over fruit salad.
bowl. Beat with rotary beater until

*See page 2

Thousand Island Dressing

Makes 1 cup   Calories: 55 per tablespoon

½   cup mayonnaise*
½   cup unsalted chili sauce
1   tablespoon finely-chopped green
    pepper
1   tablespoon finely-chopped celery

¼   teaspoon onion powder
dash pepper
1   hard-cooked egg white,
     finely-chopped, optional

Combine all ingredients. Mix well and
chill.

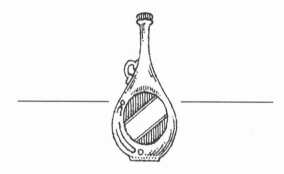

Vinaigrette Dressing

Makes 1 cup   Calories: 55 per tablespoon

⅓   cup oil
2   tablespoons lemon juice
2   tablespoons tarragon vinegar
1   teaspoon chopped fresh parsley or
½   teaspoon dry parsley flakes
½   teaspoon pepper

¼   teaspoon dry mustard powder
⅛   teaspoon garlic powder
1   hard-cooked egg white,
    finely-chopped, optional
1   tablespoon low-fat yogurt,
    optional

Place all ingredients in a jar and shake
vigorously. Chill. Serve with cooked or

raw chilled vegetables or with fresh
tomato slices.

*See page 2

Blender Mayonnaise

Makes 1 cup

Calories: 125 per tablespoon

1	egg yolk
1	tablespoon vinegar
dash	paprika
¼	teaspoon dry mustard powder

¼	teaspoon sugar
⅛	teaspoon garlic powder
1	cup oil
1	tablespoon lemon juice

Combine all ingredients except oil and lemon juice in blender container. Blend until mixed thoroughly. With blender on a low speed, pour half of the oil very slowly in a thin stream into egg mixture.

Stop blender and use rubber spatula to scrape down sides. Add lemon juice and blend. With blender running at a low speed, slowly pour remainder of oil into container. Store in refrigerator.

Breads

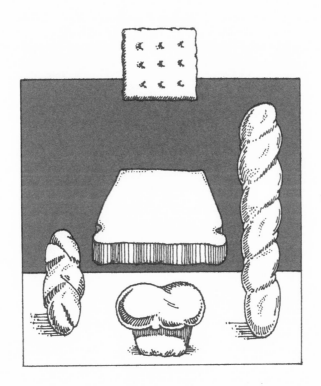

Breads

Although most yeast breads contain some sodium and saturated fat, generally they are acceptable for someone on a lower-sodium, fat-modified diet. It is not necessary to eat bread made without salt unless your doctor has given you specific instructions. If you enjoy baking, you can have a wide variety of breads and bake them at home without salt.

Use any kind of flour or combination of flours — enriched white, whole wheat, rye, soy or cornmeal. Avoid self-rising flours though, since they contain salt and a sodium-based leavening agent. As with other foods, flavor can be added to the breads by using spices, herbs, fresh or dried fruits, unsalted nuts, onion, garlic or toasted wheat germ.

If you decide to bake your own bread, you should note that yeast breads made without salt will rise more quickly than normal bread dough. If allowed to rise too much, the bread will be coarse and have a strong, yeasty taste. You can guard against this by punching the dough with two fingers when it is rising in the bowl. If you see that the indentation remains and the dough no longer springs back, then it is ready to be shaped. You should allow loaves and rolls to rise only until slightly less than double in size before placing them in the oven.

Since ready-to-eat or packaged mixes of muffins, biscuits, pancakes, waffles and nut breads contain significant amounts of sodium, cholesterol and/or saturated fat, you should avoid them. It's easy to make these breads at home by omitting the salt and using the appropriate ingredients. See page 15 for ingredient substitutions.

When you make your own baked products, remember that baked goods made without salt tend to become moldy more quickly. Therefore, when you prepare enough for several meals, freeze the unused portions. After thawing, a few minutes in the oven will make them as fresh as the day they were made.

White Bread

Makes 2 large loaves
18 slices per loaf

Calories: 75 per slice

1	package dry yeast
¼	cup lukewarm water
3	tablespoons sugar
2	tablespoons oil

1¾	cups skim milk, scalded and cooled to lukewarm
5-5½	cups all-purpose flour

Soak yeast in water for 5 minutes without stirring. In a large bowl, combine sugar, oil and milk. Add dissolved yeast. Stir in 3 cups of flour and beat until smooth. Gradually add more flour until mixture becomes stiff enough to handle. With some of remaining flour, lightly dust a clean, dry board or table top. Knead dough until smooth and elastic using small amounts of remaining flour. Place kneaded dough into a large oiled bowl, turning dough to coat entire surface with oil. Cover loosely and let rise in a warm place until almost doubled in size, or when pressed with two fingers, an indentation remains in dough. Punch dough down, cut into desired portions for loaves or rolls and let rest for 3-5 minutes. Coat two 9 x 5 x 3-inch loaf pans with oil or margarine*. Divide dough into 2 equal parts. Roll each piece into a rectangle 9 x 12 inches. Starting with the narrow side, roll dough up tightly, seal ends by pinching together and place seam side down in prepared pans. Cover loosely and let rise in a warm place until sides of dough reach top of pan, 30-45 minutes. Bake in preheated 425°F. oven 25-30 minutes. Remove loaves from pans immediately and cool on a rack. For a soft crust, brush tops of hot loaves with oil or margarine*.

White Bread

Variations: **Dinner Rolls** — Divide dough into 2 parts. Roll out 1 part and divide into 12 equal sections. Shape each into round ball and place on oiled baking sheet with sides touching for soft rolls or 1½ inches apart for crusty rolls. Let rise until almost doubled in size. Bake in preheated 425°F. oven 15-20 minutes until brown. Remove from pan and cool on a rack. For a soft crust, brush while hot with oil or margarine*.

*See page 2

Whole Wheat Bread — Use 4 cups whole wheat or graham flour and 1-1½ cups all-purpose flour in place of the all-purpose flour called for in the recipe. Three tablespoons molasses may be used in place of sugar.

Rye Bread — Use 2½ cups rye flour and 2½-3 cups all-purpose flour in place of the all-purpose flour called for in the recipe. Use ¼ cup dark molasses in place of sugar. If desired, 1 tablespoon caraway seeds may be added. Dough will not rise as much as white bread dough. Round loaves may be formed and baked on oiled baking sheets.

Herb Bread — Many different seeds, herbs or herb combinations may be used with white bread recipes. Add any of the following to dough mixture with the first addition of flour: 1 teaspoon sage and 1 tablespoon caraway seeds; 1 tablespoon oregano and 1 teaspoon basil; 1 tablespoon dill seed and 2 tablespoons grated onion; or ¼ cup each finely-chopped fresh chives and parsley.

Raisin Bread — Add 1 cup seedless raisins to white dough mixture during first addition of flour.

Cinnamon Bread — Prepare White Bread recipe. Divide dough into 2 equal parts and roll each piece into a rectangle 9 x 12 inches. For each loaf, brush dough with 2 teaspoons oil and a mixture of ¼ cup sugar and 1 teaspoon cinnamon. Roll and seal as directed for White Bread.

Swedish Bread — Increase sugar in White Bread recipe to ⅓ cup. Add 4 shelled, pulverized cardamom seeds, ½ cup finely-chopped dried apricots and ¾ cup seedless raisins to white dough mixture during first addition of flour.

Cinnamon Rolls — Prepare White Bread recipe. Divide dough into 2 equal parts and roll into rectangles about ¼-inch thick. Mix 1 cup packed brown sugar, 1 tablespoon cinnamon and 1 cup chopped walnuts. Brush dough with ¼ cup melted margarine* and sprinkle with brown sugar mixture. Roll the dough tightly into cylinders and cut in 1-inch slices. Place cut side up with sides touching on oiled baking sheet. Allow to rise until almost doubled in size, about 35 minutes. Bake in preheated 400°F. oven 30-35 minutes or until golden brown. Invert on rack to cool. While warm, drizzle with a glaze made by mixing 1 cup powdered sugar, 1 teaspoon vanilla and 1-2 tablespoons water.

*See page 2

Biscuits

Makes 12 biscuits

Calories: 130 per biscuit

2	cups all-purpose flour
1	tablespoon baking powder*

⅓	cup oil
⅔	cup skim milk

Mix flour and baking powder in bowl. Combine oil and milk and pour all at once into dry ingredients. Stir until mixture clings together and forms a ball. Knead on waxed paper 18-20 times without using additional flour. Gently pat or roll out until dough is ½ inch thick. Cut with 2-inch round cutter and place close together with edges touching on ungreased baking sheet. Bake in preheated 450°F. oven 12-15 minutes.

Variations: **Herb-Seasoned Biscuits** — Add one or more of the following to the flour mixture: 1 teaspoon garlic powder; 1 teaspoon onion powder; 2 teaspoons parsley flakes; 2 teaspoons dill weed; ½ teaspoon sage.
Drop Biscuits — Add 2 additional tablespoons skim milk and stir dough until well mixed. Drop by spoonfuls onto ungreased baking sheet.

Corn Muffins

Calories: 150 per muffin

Makes 8 large muffins

1	cup all-purpose flour
1	tablespoon sugar, optional
¾	cup yellow or white cornmeal
2	teaspoons baking powder*

2	egg whites, slightly beaten
1	cup skim milk
2	tablespoons oil

Sift flour, sugar, cornmeal and baking powder together. Combine egg whites, milk and oil and pour all at once into dry ingredients. Stir just enough to blend. Pour batter into oiled muffin tins ⅔ full, bake in preheated 425°F. oven 20-22 minutes until golden brown. Allow muffins to cool 2 minutes before removing from pan.
Variation: **Corn Bread** — Pour batter into oiled 8-inch square baking pan and bake as above.

*See page 2

Streusel-Filled Coffee Cake

Makes 9 servings

Calories: 295 per serving

Streusel Filling

    2   tablespoons margarine*, melted
    ½   cup packed brown sugar
    2   tablespoons all-purpose flour

    2   teaspoons cinnamon
    ½   cup chopped walnuts

Mix melted margarine, brown sugar, flour, cinnamon and walnuts to form the streusel filling. Set aside.

Cake Batter

    ¼   cup margarine*
    ¾   cup sugar
    2   egg whites

    ½   cup skim milk
    1½ cups sifted all-purpose flour
    2   teaspoons baking powder*

Cream margarine with sugar. Add egg whites and beat well. Add milk and mix. Sift flour and baking powder together. Add to batter and beat. Spread half the batter in a lightly-oiled 9-inch square baking pan. Sprinkle with half of streusel filling. Add remaining batter and sprinkle with remaining filling. Bake in preheated 375°F. oven 25-35 minutes. Serve warm.

*See page 2

Banana Bread

Makes 16 servings

Calories: 130 per serving

⅓ cup oil
⅔ cup sugar
1 cup mashed ripe banana (2-3 medium bananas)

1¾ cups sifted all-purpose flour
2 teaspoons baking powder*
3 egg whites

Beat oil and ⅓ cup sugar together. Add banana and mix well. Sift flour and baking powder together, add to batter and beat. In a separate bowl, beat egg whites until foamy. Gradually add ⅓ cup sugar and beat until egg whites form soft peaks. Fold egg whites into the batter. Pour into lightly-oiled 5 x 9-inch loaf pan and bake in preheated 350°F. oven 55 minutes. Remove from oven and allow to stand 10 minutes. Invert bread on a wire rack to cool.

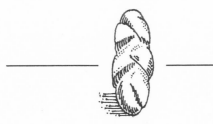

Seasoned Croutons

Makes 2 cups

Calories: 85 per ¼ cup

¼ cup margarine*, softened
½ teaspoon onion powder
¼ teaspoon garlic powder

¼ teaspoon dill weed
⅛ teaspoon pepper
4 slices bread*

Add seasonings to margarine and mix well. Spread margarine mixture on one side of each slice of bread. Cut bread into half-inch cubes. Spread on cookie sheet and bake in 300°F. oven 15-20 minutes until crisp and dry. Cool and store in tightly-covered container. Use as a garnish for soups or salads.

*See page 2

75

Marmalade Coffee Cake

Makes 9 servings

Calories: 290 per serving

Marmalade Topping

¼ cup sugar
¼ cup all-purpose flour

1 tablespoon water
½ cup marmalade

Mix sugar with flour; add water and marmalade and mix well, set aside.

Cake Batter

2 cups sifted all-purpose flour
½ cup sugar
1½ teaspoons baking powder*
1 teaspoon grated orange peel

2 egg whites, slightly beaten
½ cup skim milk
½ cup orange juice
⅓ cup oil

Sift flour, sugar and baking powder together. Combine all other ingredients and quickly stir into flour mixture. Stir only enough to mix ingredients. Batter will appear lumpy. Pour into a lightly-oiled 9-inch square baking pan. Spread marmalade topping evenly over the top. Bake in preheated 375°F. oven 25-35 minutes. Serve plain or with Mock Whipped Cream, page 108.

*See page 2

Pancakes

Makes 15 4-inch pancakes

Calories: 90 per pancake

1½   cups all-purpose flour
2   tablespoons sugar
1   tablespoon baking powder*
¼   teaspoon cinnamon

1   egg white
¼   cup oil
1½   cups skim milk
½   teaspoon vanilla

Sift dry ingredients together in a bowl. Beat egg white until foamy. Mix in oil, milk and vanilla. Add to dry ingredients. Beat only until batter is smooth. Spoon batter onto lightly-oiled preheated griddle or skillet. When bubbles form and begin to break, turn and brown on other side. May be served with margarine* and syrup. Leftover pancakes may be layered between waxed paper and frozen. Reheat in toaster when needed.

Variations: **Blueberry Pancakes** — Add ½ cup blueberries to batter.
Nut Pancakes — Add ¼ cup chopped walnuts to batter.
Wheat Germ Pancakes — Add ½ cup toasted wheat germ to batter.

Blueberry Muffins

Makes 12 muffins

Calories: 135 per muffin

1   cup blueberries, fresh or frozen
1¾   cups all-purpose flour
2½   teaspoons baking powder*
⅓   cup sugar

2   egg whites, slightly beaten
¼   cup oil
½   cup skim milk
1   teaspoon sugar

Wash and drain fresh or frozen berries. Sift flour, baking powder and ⅓ cup sugar together. Combine egg whites, oil and milk and pour all at once into dry ingredients. Stir just enough to blend. Gently stir in blueberries. Pour batter into oiled muffin tins ⅔ full. Sprinkle lightly with 1 teaspoon sugar and bake in preheated 400°F. oven 20-25 minutes or until browned. Allow muffins to cool 2 minutes before removing from pan.

*See page 2

Crepes

Makes 22 6-inch crepes

Calories: 60 per crepe

¾ cup skim milk
¾ cup cold water
2 egg whites
1½ cups sifted all-purpose flour

⅓ cup margarine*, melted
2 tablespoons rum or orange liqueur
1 tablespoon sugar
4 drops yellow food coloring

Beat all ingredients together. Cover and refrigerate for 2 hours or overnight. Batter will be thin. Brush a small iron skillet or teflon pan lightly with oil. Place over moderate heat. Pour 2 tablespoons batter in center of preheated skillet. Tilt pan in all directions until batter covers bottom of pan. Return to heat for about 1 minute. Shake pan sharply to loosen crepe. Lift edges with a spatula and turn the crepe over when lightly browned. Brown lightly, approximately ½ minute, on the other side. If first crepe appears too thick, beat in 2-3 tablespoons additional water. Lightly oil pan and proceed with remaining batter. Crepes may be stacked and refrigerated overnight or frozen with waxed paper between each. Crepes should be at room temperature for ease in rolling. May be used with recipes on pages 39, 98 and 99 or they may be rolled without a filling. Brush rolled crepes with margarine*, warm in oven and serve topped with maple syrup, powdered sugar or cinnamon-sugar.

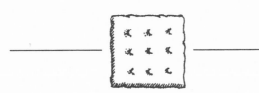

*See page 2

Soups and Sauces

Soups and Sauces

When reducing the sodium content of your diet, you may find the preparation of soups and sauces one of your biggest challenges. This is especially true since canned, dried and frozen soups or soup mixes are among the saltiest convenience foods available. However, there are tasty alternatives.

Broths or soups should be prepared without adding salt, regular bouillon cubes or prepared flavoring packets. Instead, use unsalted bouillon cubes or the recipes in this section. See page 13 for further suggestions about seasoning soups.

You can remove the fat from homemade soup by preparing it a day in advance and chilling it overnight in the refrigerator. When you do this, you are allowing the fat to rise to the top and harden, making it easy to remove. If you can't prepare the broth in advance, the next best technique is to skim off as much fat as possible with a large spoon. Remove the remaining fat by floating a paper towel on top of the hot soup and removing it when the fat is absorbed. Then you may add vegetables, macaroni or rice to the broth.

You can make cream soups, chowders and sauces from a basic white sauce of flour, margarine and skim milk, omitting salt. Many kinds of soups may be prepared by adding pureed or chopped vegetables, seafood and your favorite herbs and spices to the basic white sauce.

Soup can be topped with Seasoned Croutons, page 75, lemon slices, low-fat yogurt, chopped onions or chives or a sprinkle of herbs. Soup can also be accompanied by soda crackers without salt sprinkled on top, unsalted pretzels or toast strips.

For tomato sauces, you may wish to use the recipes in this book or you can use fresh or canned tomatoes, unsalted tomato paste or unsalted tomato puree as a base with other seasonings in place of salt.

Several of the soup and sauce recipes in this cookbook yield large quantities. It may be helpful to freeze meal-sized portions in separate containers.

Beef Broth

Makes 3 cups

Calories: 10 per cup

1 tablespoon oil
1 pound boneless, lean beef shank, well-trimmed
1 quart water
1 small onion, chopped
1 bay leaf

4 peppercorns
4 whole cloves
½ teaspoon garlic powder
⅛ teaspoon thyme
⅛ teaspoon marjoram

Heat oil in large saucepan. Brown meat lightly and pour off fat. Add remaining ingredients. Bring to a boil. Cover, reduce heat and simmer 2-2½ hours or until meat is tender. Remove meat from broth, refrigerate and use in another recipe. Strain and measure broth. Adjust yield to 3 cups either by adding water or boiling down excess broth. Refrigerate broth. When ready to use, remove and discard hardened fat from surface of broth. Heat.

Variation: **Beef Vegetable Soup** — Add ¼-½ cup of any or all of the following chopped, fresh vegetables to broth: cabbage, carrots, celery, onion, green beans and tomatoes. Simmer 20-30 minutes. Cut half of meat into bite-size pieces and add to vegetable soup. Use remaining meat for sandwiches or other recipes.

Cream of Asparagus Soup

Makes 3 servings

Calories: 135 per serving

1 cup fresh or frozen chopped asparagus, cooked, reserving ½ cup cooking liquid
2 tablespoons margarine*
2 tablespoons all-purpose flour

½ teaspoon onion powder
⅛ teaspoon pepper
1 cup skim milk
2 tablespoons dry white table wine
dash paprika

Mix asparagus in a blender or force it through a fine strainer and set aside. Melt margarine in saucepan. Add flour, onion powder and pepper. Cook and mix well. Gradually add milk, stirring constantly. Add ½ cup reserved vegetable liquid.

Cook over medium heat, stirring until slightly thickened. Add asparagus; heat through. Shortly before serving, add wine and sprinkle with paprika.

Variation: **Cream of Broccoli Soup** — Use broccoli in place of asparagus.

*See page 2

Chicken Broth

Makes 3 cups

Calories: 15 per cup

2½ pound frying chicken, cut in pieces, skinned
1 quart water
1 medium onion, chopped
8 whole cloves
2 bay leaves

½ teaspoon pepper
¼ teaspoon marjoram
¼ teaspoon rosemary
¼ teaspoon basil
⅛ teaspoon garlic powder

Place chicken in large, deep pan. Add remaining ingredients. Bring to a boil. Cover, reduce heat and simmer 2½ hours or until chicken is tender. Remove chicken from broth, refrigerate and use in another recipe. Strain and measure broth. Adjust yield to 3 cups either by adding water or cooking down excess broth. Refrigerate broth. When ready to use, remove and discard hardened fat from surface of broth. Heat.

Variations: **Turkey Broth** — 1½ pounds raw turkey may be substituted for chicken. **Chicken Rice Soup** — Cut half of chicken into bite-size pieces and add to broth with ½ cup cooked rice. Use remaining chicken for sandwiches or other recipes.

Split Pea Soup

Makes 6 servings

Calories: 75 per serving

1 cup (½ pound) dried split peas
2 quarts water
1 carrot, chopped
2 stalks celery, chopped
1 medium onion, chopped
½ teaspoon unsalted liquid smoke

1 tablespoon chopped fresh parsley or 1½ teaspoons dry parsley flakes
¼ teaspoon onion powder
⅛ teaspoon garlic powder
⅛ teaspoon pepper

Place all ingredients in large pan. Cover and simmer 2½-3 hours. If soup becomes too thick, add more water. If a smooth soup is desired, mix in a blender or force through a sieve.

Hamburger – Vegetable Soup

Makes 8 servings

Calories: 170 per serving

1½ pounds lean ground beef
1 can (10 ounces) tomatoes*
1 can (8 ounces) unsalted tomato juice
1 cup chopped onion
¼ cup thinly-sliced fresh carrots
1 cup diced raw potatoes
1 cup chopped cabbage
1 cup diced green pepper
1 package (10 ounces) frozen cut green beans

1 package (10 ounces) frozen whole kernel corn
1 bay leaf
½ teaspoon basil
¼ teaspoon dill weed
¼ teaspoon pepper
¼ teaspoon thyme
½ teaspoon garlic powder
6 cups water

Brown meat in large skillet. Pour off fat. Add remaining ingredients. Bring mixture to a boil. Reduce heat, cover and simmer 1 hour or until vegetables are tender. Stir occasionally. Remove bay leaf before serving.

Onion Soup

Makes 3 servings

Calories: 185 per serving

2 tablespoons margarine*, melted
1 tablespoon oil
2 medium onions, sliced
⅛ teaspoon sugar
2 teaspoons all-purpose flour
2½ cups water

2 unsalted beef bouillon cubes
2 tablespoons vermouth or dry white table wine
⅛ teaspoon pepper
1 slice bread*, toasted and cut into cubes

Combine margarine, oil and onions in saucepan. Cover and cook over low heat 15 minutes. Add sugar and cook uncovered 10 minutes, stirring occasionally, until the onions are a deep, golden brown. Mix in flour. Stir in water. Add bouillon cubes, vermouth and pepper and simmer 15-30 minutes. Place soup in cups and top with Seasoned Croutons, page 75, or cubes of toast.

*See page 2

83

Mock Sour Cream

Makes 2 cups

Calories: 10 per tablespoon

1½   cups (12 ounces) unsalted dry cottage cheese
½   cup skim milk

1   tablespoon lemon juice
¼   teaspoon onion powder

Mix all ingredients in a blender until smooth and creamy. Chill.

Catsup

Makes 1 quart

Calories: 20 per tablespoon

3   cans (6 ounces each) unsalted tomato paste
4   cups water
½   cup chopped onion
½   cup chopped celery
½   cup vinegar
½   cup sugar
1   tablespoon packed brown sugar
2   tablespoons margarine*

1   teaspoon molasses
⅛   teaspoon cloves
⅛   teaspoon cinnamon
⅛   teaspoon basil
⅛   teaspoon tarragon
⅛   teaspoon pepper
⅛   teaspoon onion powder
⅛   teaspoon garlic powder

Mix tomato paste, water, onion, celery, vinegar and sugar in a blender until mixture is smooth. If blender is not available use a mixer but strain catsup at the end of the cooking period. Place tomato mixture and remaining ingredients in saucepan and simmer uncovered for 1½ hours or until catsup is thickened and reduced to one half original volume. Stir occasionally. May be stored in refrigerator for one month. For longer storage, freeze in small quantities and thaw in refrigerator as needed.

*See page 2

Chili Sauce

Makes 3 cups

Calories: 20 per tablespoon

- 2 cans (16 ounces each) unsalted tomato puree
- ½ cup chopped onion
- ½ cup vinegar
- ½ cup sugar
- ½ cup chopped celery
- ½ medium green pepper, chopped
- 2 tablespoons margarine*
- 1 tablespoon lemon juice

- 1 teaspoon brown sugar
- ½ teaspoon molasses
- ¼ teaspoon hot pepper sauce
- ⅛ teaspoon cloves
- ⅛ teaspoon cinnamon
- ⅛ teaspoon pepper
- ⅛ teaspoon basil
- ⅛ teaspoon tarragon

Mix all ingredients in 3-quart saucepan. Bring to a boil, then reduce heat and simmer uncovered 1½ hours or until sauce is thickened and reduced to one half original volume. Stir occasionally. May be stored in refrigerator for one month. For longer storage, freeze in small quantities for use as needed.

Chili Powder*

Makes 4 tablespoons

Calories: 10 per teaspoon

- 3 tablespoons paprika
- 2 teaspoons finely crushed oregano
- 1 teaspoon ground cumin

- 1 teaspoon ground turmeric
- 1 teaspoon garlic powder
- ¼ teaspoon cayenne pepper

Mix all ingredients together thoroughly and use in place of chili powder.

Horseradish Sauce

Makes 1½ cups

Calories: 5 per tablespoon

- ½ medium (6 ounces) horseradish root, peeled

- ½ cup white vinegar

Cut horseradish into cubes and chop in blender with vinegar until desired consistency or finely grate horseradish and mix with vinegar. Keep refrigerated.

*See page 2

Tomato Sauce

Makes 1 quart

Calories: 20 per ¼ cup

2 cans (6 ounces each) unsalted tomato paste
3 cups water
¼ cup finely-chopped onion
1 garlic clove, minced

2 tablespoons lemon juice
dash hot pepper sauce
¼ teaspoon basil
⅛ teaspoon pepper

Combine all ingredients and mix well. Simmer over low heat for 30 minutes. Stir occasionally. Use in any recipe requiring unsalted tomato sauce. May be stored in refrigerator for one week. For longer storage, freeze in small quantities for use as needed.

Chunky Tomato Sauce

Makes 1 cup

Calories: 80 per ¼ cup

1 tablespoon chopped onion
1 tablespoon chopped green pepper
2 tablespoons margarine*
1 tablespoon all-purpose flour

1¼ cups chopped, peeled fresh tomatoes or 1 cup canned tomatoes*
dash pepper

Cook onion and green pepper in margarine until tender. Stir in flour until well blended. Add chopped tomatoes and cook, stirring constantly until tomatoes are tender and sauce is thickened. Add pepper.

Lemon – Parsley Sauce

Makes ⅔ cup

Calories: 75 per tablespoon

½ cup margarine*, melted
2 tablespoons fresh lemon juice
1 tablespoon chopped, fresh parsley

1 teaspoon grated lemon peel
dash paprika

Combine margarine and lemon juice. Add parsley, lemon peel and paprika. Serve warm over poached, baked or broiled fish.

*See page 2

Barbecue Sauce

Makes 1 quart

Calories: 60 per ¼ cup

2 cans (6 ounces each) unsalted tomato paste
2 cups water
½ cup unsalted catsup
¼ cup packed brown sugar
2 tablespoons lemon juice
¼ cup chopped onion
1 garlic clove, minced

2 tablespoons chili powder*
2 tablespoons vinegar
2 tablespoons oil
1 tablespoon chopped parsley
1 teaspoon dry mustard powder
1 teaspoon paprika
⅛ teaspoon pepper
dash hot pepper sauce, optional

Combine all ingredients in a saucepan and mix well. Simmer uncovered over low heat 20 minutes. May be stored in refrigerator for one month. For longer storage, freeze in small quantities for use as needed.

Swedish Dill Sauce

Makes 2 servings

Calories: 45 per serving

½ teaspoon dry mustard powder
½ teaspoon water
1½ teaspoons onion flakes or 1 tablespoon finely-chopped onion

1 teaspoon dill weed
1 tablespoon vinegar
¼ cup chopped peeled cucumber
½ cup low-fat plain yogurt

Combine mustard and water in small mixing bowl. Let stand 10 minutes. Add remaining ingredients. Mix thoroughly. Serve cold as accompaniment for hot or chilled fish. May also be used as a dip for raw vegetables or as a dressing for sliced cucumbers.

*See page 2

Herbed Margarine

Makes ¼ cup

Calories: 100 per tablespoon

¼ cup margarine*
1 teaspoon marjoram
½ teaspoon tarragon
⅛ teaspoon basil

⅛ teaspoon dry parsley flakes
dash dill weed
dash fennel seed, crushed

Combine and mix thoroughly. Use as a spread for bread or toast, or as a topping for vegetables.

Mushroom Sauce

Makes 2 cups

Calories: 20 per tablespoon

¼ cup chopped onion
½ pound fresh mushrooms, sliced
¼ cup margarine*
1 tablespoon all-purpose flour

⅛ teaspoon pepper
⅛ teaspoon garlic powder
2 cups skim milk
1 tablespoon dry white table wine

Cook onion and mushrooms in margarine until tender. Add flour, pepper and garlic powder and mix well. Gradually add milk, stirring constantly. Cook over medium heat, stirring until thickened. Stir in wine.

Hot Prepared Mustard

Makes ½ cup

Calories: 35 per tablespoon

2 tablespoons dry mustard powder
2 tablespoons sugar
¼ cup all-purpose flour
¼ teaspoon onion powder

¼ teaspoon turmeric
2 tablespoons lemon juice
2 tablespoons water

Sift dry ingredients together or stir until evenly blended. Add lemon juice and water. Place in covered container and refrigerate.

*See page 2

Desserts

Desserts

Fruit is the perfect dessert. It can be served in literally hundreds of ways; it's low in calories; and it contains no sodium, cholesterol or fat.

A fun variation is to make dessert kabobs with fresh fruit served on small skewers. Strawberries, pineapple chunks, grapes and melon balls make a nice combination.

Canned fruit served attractively in a parfait glass is another alternative. Texture and color can be added by using cubes of red-skinned apples. As a topping, try a tablespoon of liqueur, then chill.

Your favorite cookbooks will have many recipes for baked, broiled or poached fruits. Generally, these recipes are acceptable because they do not call for salt. If you discover butter or shortening listed as an ingredient, use margarine instead.

Gelatin desserts can be prepared plain or with fruit. To enhance the flavor, substitute an equal amount of fruit juice for water. You can mold your gelatin desserts into various shapes or cut them into cubes and top with Mock Whipped Cream, page 108.

Because ice cream contains significant amounts of fat and cholesterol, you should learn to substitute frozen yogurt, sherbert or ice milk.

Other desserts such as cakes, pies and cookies contain significant amounts of sodium, fat and cholesterol. You can prepare them yourself, however, and still adhere to a lower-sodium, fat-modified diet by following the recipes in this cookbook or by adapting your own recipes using our guidelines.

Pineapple Upside-Down Cake

Makes 8 servings

Calories: 365 per serving

⅔ cup margarine*
½ cup packed brown sugar
1 can (14½ ounces) sliced pineapple, drained
¾ cup sugar

¾ teaspoon vanilla
1⅓ cups sifted cake flour
1½ teaspoons baking powder*
½ cup ice water
2 egg whites

Melt ⅓ cup margarine in a 9-inch round cake pan. Sprinkle with brown sugar and arrange pineapple in pan. In a separate bowl, cream remaining margarine with ⅓ cup sugar. Add vanilla. Sift flour and baking powder together. Add to margarine mixture alternately with ice water, beating well after each addition. In separate bowl, beat egg whites until foamy. Gradually add remaining sugar and beat until egg whites form soft peaks. Fold egg whites into batter. Pour into cake pan and bake in preheated 350°F. oven 50-55 minutes. Remove from oven and allow to stand 10 minutes. Invert cake on a wire rack to cool.

Applesauce Cake

Makes 9 servings

Calories: 335 per serving

½ cup margarine*
1 cup sugar
2 egg whites
1½ cups applesauce
2 cups all-purpose flour

1½ teaspoons baking powder*
1 teaspoon cloves
1 teaspoon nutmeg
2 teaspoons cinnamon
½ cup raisins

Cream margarine with sugar until fluffy. Add egg whites and beat well. Add applesauce and beat. Sift dry ingredients together, add to margarine mixture and mix well. Stir in raisins. Pour into lightly-oiled 9-inch square cake pan and bake in preheated 350°F. oven 45 minutes. Serve warm.

*See page 2

White Cake

Makes 12 servings

Calories: 245 per serving
Calories: 415 per serving
with White Cream Frosting

2¼	cups sifted cake flour
1	tablespoon baking powder*
1¼	cups sugar
½	cup oil

¾	cup skim milk
1	teaspoon vanilla
3	egg whites

Sift flour, baking powder and ¾ cup of sugar together. Make a well in the dry ingredients and add oil, ½ cup milk and vanilla. Mix until well combined, then beat 1 additional minute at medium speed of mixer or 150 strokes by hand. Batter will be very thick. Add remaining milk and mix 1 more minute at medium speed of mixer or 150 strokes by hand. In a separate bowl, beat egg whites until foamy. Gradually add remaining sugar, beating until egg whites form soft peaks. Fold egg whites gently into batter. Pour into 2 lightly-oiled and floured 8-inch cake pans or into cupcake tins. Bake in preheated 375°F. oven 20-30 minutes for layer cake or 15-20 minutes for cupcakes or until cake springs back when touched lightly. Allow to cool 10 minutes. Then remove from pan and complete cooling on a rack. May frost with White Cream Frosting, below.

Variations: **Yellow Cake** – Add ⅛ teaspoon yellow food coloring to batter. **Orange Cake** – Use ⅔ cup orange juice and 1 tablespoon lemon juice in place of milk. Add 1 tablespoon grated orange peel to dry ingredients. **Spice Cake** – Add 1 teaspoon cinnamon, 1 teaspoon cloves and ½ teaspoon allspice to dry ingredients.

White Cream Frosting

Makes frosting for 8- or 9-inch layer cake

Calories: 170 per serving

3	tablespoons all-purpose flour
¾	cup skim milk
¾	cup margarine*

1¼	cups powdered sugar
1	teaspoon vanilla

Mix flour and milk in small saucepan. Cook, stirring constantly until mixture boils and thickens. Cool. Cream margarine with sugar and vanilla until light and fluffy, about 10 minutes. Add cooled flour mixture and beat until smooth.

*See page 2

Chocolate Cake

Makes 16 servings

Calories: 235 per serving
360 per serving
with White Cream
Frosting

2½   cups all-purpose flour
⅓   cup cocoa
3½   teaspoons baking powder*
⅔   cup oil
¾   cup water
½   cup skim milk
1   teaspoon vanilla
4   egg whites
¼   teaspoon cream of tartar
1¾   cups sugar

Lightly oil 2 9-inch cake pans. Line pans with waxed paper cut to fit the bottom of each pan. Sift flour, cocoa and baking powder together. In a separate bowl mix oil, water, milk and vanilla together. Add to flour mixture and beat until well combined. Batter will resemble a thick paste. Beat egg whites until foamy. Add cream of tartar and gradually add sugar, beating until egg whites form soft peaks. Fold egg whites into batter. Pour into prepared pans and bake in preheated 375°F. oven 25-30 minutes. May frost with White Cream Frosting, page 92.

Angel Food Cake

Makes 12 servings

Calories: 130 per serving

1   cup sifted cake flour
1¼   cups sugar
1¼   cups (10-12) egg whites, room temperature
1   teaspoon cream of tartar
½   teaspoon vanilla
½   teaspoon almond extract

Sift flour and ½ cup sugar together 3 times. Beat egg whites until foamy. Add cream of tartar, vanilla and almond extract. Continue beating until soft, moist, glossy peaks form. Gradually add remaining sugar and continue beating at high speed until volume increases and stiff peaks form. By hand, gently fold in sifted flour-sugar mixture only until all flour is moistened. Pour into 9-inch tube pan. Cut through batter carefully with a thin spatula to break up large air pockets. Bake in preheated 350°F. oven 40-45 minutes. Remove from oven and invert pan for 1½ hours or until cold. Remove from pan before storing.

*See page 2

Denver Chocolate Pudding Cake

Calories: 250 per serving

Makes 9 servings

1	cup all-purpose flour
¾	cup sugar
2	teaspoons baking powder*
3	tablespoons margarine*, melted
3	tablespoons cocoa
½	cup skim milk

½	teaspoon vanilla
½	cup packed brown sugar
½	cup sugar
¼	cup cocoa
1½	cups cold water or coffee

Sift flour, ¾ cup sugar and baking powder together in a bowl. Combine margarine and 3 tablespoons cocoa and add to dry ingredients. Beat in milk and vanilla. Pour into lightly oiled 9-inch square baking pan. Sprinkle remaining dry ingredients over the top of the batter one at a time but do not mix. Pour water (or coffee) over the top. Bake in a preheated 350°F. oven 40 minutes. To serve, invert each piece on dessert plate. Serve plain or with Mock Whipped Cream, page 108.

Lemon Nut Cookies

Makes 2 dozen cookies

Calories: 90 per cookie

½	cup margarine*
½	cup sugar
1	egg, separated
1	teaspoon vanilla
2	tablespoons fresh lemon juice

2	teaspoons grated lemon peel
2	teaspoons grated orange peel
1¼	cups sifted all-purpose flour
½	cup finely-chopped walnuts

Cream margarine with sugar. Add egg yolk, vanilla, lemon juice and grated lemon and orange peels and beat. Add flour and mix well. Chill one hour. Dip a teaspoonful of dough into slightly-beaten egg white and then into nuts. Place nut side up, 2 inches apart on lightly-oiled cookie sheet. Bake in preheated 350°F. oven 20-25 minutes or until lightly browned. Transfer to cooling rack immediately.

*See page 2

Oatmeal Cookies

Makes 2½ dozen cookies

Calories: 70 per cookie

½ cup margarine*
½ cup packed brown sugar
1 tablespoon water

¼ teaspoon vanilla
1½ cups all-purpose flour
1 cup uncooked oatmeal

Cream margarine with sugar. Stir in water and vanilla. Add flour, mixing well. Stir in oatmeal. Form dough into 1-inch balls and place 2 inches apart on lightly-oiled cookie sheet. Flatten with a fork which has been dipped in flour. Bake in preheated 350°F. oven 15 minutes or until lightly browned. Transfer to cooling rack immediately.

Peanut Butter Cookies

Makes 4 dozen cookies

Calories: 75 per cookie

½ cup margarine*
½ cup sugar
½ cup packed brown sugar
1 egg

1 cup peanut butter*
½ teaspoon vanilla
1½ cups all-purpose flour
1¼ teaspoons baking powder*

Cream margarine with sugar and brown sugar. Stir in egg. Add peanut butter and vanilla and beat. Sift flour and baking powder together. Add to margarine mixture and mix well. Form dough into 1½-inch balls and place 3 inches apart on lightly-oiled cookie sheet. Flatten with a fork. Bake in preheated 350°F. oven 15 minutes or until done. Allow cookies to cool 2-3 minutes on cookie sheet before transferring to cooling rack.

*See page 2

Walnut Cocoons

Makes 2 dozen cookies

Calories: 95 per cookie

1½ cups all-purpose flour
2 tablespoons powdered sugar
½ cup margarine*
1 cup finely-chopped walnuts

1 teaspoon vanilla
3 tablespoons cold water,
  approximately
  powdered sugar

Sift flour and sugar together into bowl. Cut in margarine with a fork or pastry blender. Mix in walnuts, vanilla and enough cold water to make a soft dough. Form into small rolls 1-inch long and ½-inch thick. Place 2 inches apart on a lightly-oiled cookie sheet. Bake in preheated 350°F. oven 25-30 minutes or until firm. While warm, roll in powdered sugar.

Date Rounds

Makes 2½ dozen cookies

Calories: 75 per cookie

½ cup margarine*
⅓ cup powdered sugar
1 tablespoon skim milk
1 teaspoon vanilla

1¼ cups sifted all-purpose flour
⅔ cup chopped dates
½ cup chopped walnuts
  powdered sugar

Cream margarine with ⅓ cup powdered sugar. Add milk and vanilla. Add flour and stir well. Mix in dates and nuts. Form dough in 1-inch balls and place 2 inches apart on ungreased cookie sheet. Bake in preheated 300°F. oven 20-25 minutes or until lightly browned. While warm, roll in powdered sugar.

*See page 2

Vanilla Cookies

Makes 4 dozen

Calories: 65 per cookie

1 cup margarine*
½ cup sugar
1 whole egg

1 egg white
½ teaspoon vanilla
2¾ cups all-purpose flour

Cream margarine with sugar. Add whole egg, egg white and vanilla and beat until mixture is a light lemon color. Add flour and mix well. Form dough in 1-inch balls and place 2 inches apart on lightly-oiled cookie sheet. Flatten with a fork. Bake in preheated 350°F. oven 10-15 minutes or until lightly browned.
Variations: **Orange Cookies** — Add 1 tablespoon grated orange peel to dough.

Thumbprint Cookies — Flatten balls only slightly. Make an indentation with thumb and fill with jelly.
Cinnamon Cookies — Mix ½ teaspoon cinnamon and ¼ cup sugar. Sprinkle on cookies before baking.
Snowball Cookies — Mix ½ cup finely chopped walnuts into dough. Do not flatten balls of dough. After baking, roll in powdered sugar.

Pralines

Makes 6 dozen cookies

Calories: 55 per cookie

1 cup margarine*
1 cup packed brown sugar
1 egg

1 tablespoon vanilla
1½ cups sifted all-purpose flour
1 cup chopped toasted pecans

Cream margarine with sugar. Add egg and vanilla and beat. Add flour and mix well. Mix in nuts. Drop by teaspoonfuls on lightly-oiled cookie sheet. Bake in preheated 350°F. oven 12 minutes or until lightly browned.

*See page 2

Popcorn Macaroons

Makes 5 dozen macaroons

Calories: 20 per macaroon

1 cup unsalted popped corn
1 cup finely-chopped walnuts
3 egg whites

1 cup powdered sugar
¾ teaspoon vanilla

Chop popped corn finely and mix with nuts. In a separate bowl beat egg whites until foamy. Gradually add sugar and continue beating until egg whites form stiff peaks. Add vanilla and beat. Fold popcorn and nut mixture into egg whites. Drop by half-teaspoonful onto lightly-oiled cookie sheet. Bake in preheated 300°F. oven 30-35 minutes. Transfer to cooling rack immediately.

Sunshine Crepes

Makes 10 Crepes

Calories: 200 per Crepe

½ recipe Crepes, page 78
⅓ cup margarine*
½ cup orange marmalade

2 tablespoons sugar
1 tablespoon cornstarch
3 large bananas, sliced

Prepare Crepes. To make filling, heat margarine and marmalade together, stirring constantly until margarine melts. Mix sugar and cornstarch together. Slowly stir into margarine mixture. Cook over medium heat, stirring constantly until mixture is smooth and bubbly. Remove from heat. Fold in bananas. Spoon banana mixture into center of 10 warm crepes. Roll. May be topped with powdered sugar or low-fat yogurt and sprinkled with nutmeg.
Variation: **Strawberry Crepes** — Place a few tablespoons vanilla ice milk in center of each crepe and roll up. Top with sliced fresh strawberries.

*See page 2

Apple-Filled Crepes

Makes 10 crepes   Calories: 135 per crepe

½ recipe Crepes, page 78
2 tablespoons margarine*
5 apples, peeled and sliced (Golden Delicious apples preferred)

¼ cup sugar
1 tablespoon lemon juice
1 teaspoon grated lemon peel
⅛ teaspoon nutmeg

Prepare Crepes. To make filling, melt margarine in large skillet. Add remaining ingredients and cook until apples are tender, stirring occasionally. Remove from heat. Spoon ⅔ of apple mixture into center of crepes. Roll. Place seam side down in a lightly-oiled baking dish. Spoon remaining apple mixture over top of crepes. Cover and bake in 325°F. oven 25 minutes or until hot. Sprinkle with powdered sugar before serving. Serve as a dessert or for brunch with Pork Sausage Patties, page 28.

Matzo Crumb Pie Crust

Makes 9-inch pie shell   Calories: 260 per ⅛ crust

1 cup unsalted matzo meal
¼ cup sugar

¼ teaspoon cinnamon, optional
¼ cup margarine*, melted

Mix matzo meal and sugar together. Add cinnamon and margarine and mix thoroughly. Press firmly into a 9-inch pie plate. Bake in 350°F. oven 20 minutes or until lightly browned. Fill with Citrus Chiffon, page 102, or a cream pie filling prepared with skim milk and without egg yolks. See pages 105 and 106 for pudding recipes.

*See page 2

Pie Crust

Makes 2 9-inch pie shells or pastry for 1 2-crust pie

Calories 260 per ⅛ crust

2¼   cups all-purpose flour
½   teaspoon sugar

⅓   cup cold skim milk
½   cup plus 1 tablespoon oil

Mix flour and sugar in bowl. Pour milk and oil into the same measuring cup. Do not stir. Add all at once to flour. Stir with fork until well mixed and then form into a smooth ball with hands. Roll out between two 12-inch squares of waxed paper using short, brisk strokes until pastry reaches edge of paper. Peel off top paper. Invert crust and place on pie plate. Carefully peel off paper and gently fit into pie plate. For 2-crust pie, place fruit filling in pie crust and top with second crust; flute edges and make slits. Sprinkle crust with 1 teaspoon sugar and bake according to filling directions. For 2 single-crust pie shells, flute the edges and prick pastry with a fork. Repeat with second crust. Bake in a preheated 450°F. oven 12-14 minutes or until lightly browned.

Cherry Pie

Makes 1 9-inch pie (8 servings)

Calories: 460 per serving

1⅓   cups sugar
⅓   cup all-purpose flour
½   teaspoon cinnamon
2   cans (1 pound each) sour cherries, drained

⅛   teaspoon almond extract
     Pie Crust, page 100
1   tablespoon margarine*

Mix dry ingredients together. Combine cherries and almond extract and add to flour mixture. Line pan with pie crust and fill with cherry mixture. Dot with margarine and top with second crust. Seal edges and make slits in top crust. Bake in preheated 425°F. oven 35-45 minutes.

Variations: **Blueberry Pie** — Use 4 cups fresh or frozen blueberries and reduce sugar to 1 cup.
Peach Pie — Use 2½ to 3 pounds (10 medium) peaches, sliced, and reduce sugar to ⅔ cup.

*See page 2

Apple Pie

Makes 1 9-inch pie (8 servings)

Calories: 460 per serving

1   cup sugar
1   teaspoon cinnamon
2½   pounds (8 medium) tart, firm
    apples, sliced
    Pie Crust, page 100
1   tablespoon margarine*

Mix dry ingredients together. Add sliced apples. Line pan with pie crust and fill with mixture. Dot with margarine and top with second crust. Seal edges and make slits in top crust. Bake in preheated 425°F. oven 35-45 minutes.

Pumpkin Pie

Makes 1 9-inch pie (8 servings)

Calories: 265 per serving

⅔   cup packed brown sugar
1   teaspoon cinnamon
½   teaspoon ginger
¼   teaspoon cloves
1½   cups (1 pound can) pumpkin*
1   can (13 ounces) evaporated skim
    milk
3   egg whites, beaten until foamy
½   recipe Pie Crust, page 100
    unbaked

Mix brown sugar, spices and pumpkin together. Add milk and egg whites and beat until thoroughly mixed. Pour into pastry-lined pan. Bake in preheated 400°F. oven 45-50 minutes or until knife inserted near center of pie comes out clean.

*See page 2

Citrus Chiffon

Makes 8 servings

Calories: 70 per serving

2 teaspoons unflavored gelatin
¼ cup cold water
½ cup hot water
½ cup sugar

2 teaspoons grated lemon peel
¾ cup orange juice
2 tablespoons lemon juice
⅓ cup non-fat dry milk powder

Sprinkle gelatin over cold water in saucepan and allow to stand 5 minutes. Add hot water and sugar. Heat, stirring constantly until gelatin is dissolved. Remove from heat. Stir in lemon peel and orange and lemon juices. Chill until thickened to the consistency of unbeaten egg white. Sprinkle milk powder over gelatin mixture. Using an electric mixer, beat until light and fluffy. Pour into a serving bowl or a 1-quart mold and chill 8 hours or overnight. Unmold or spoon into serving dishes. Serve with fresh strawberries or orange slices.

Variation: **Citrus Chiffon Pie** – Prepare 1½ recipes of Citrus Chiffon. Pour into 9-inch baked Pie Crust, page 100, or Matzo Crumb Pie Crust, page 99. Top with Mock Whipped Cream, page 108.

Baked Pears

Makes 4 servings

Calories: 100 per serving

¼ cup water
¼ cup sugar
4 lemon slices

¼ teaspoon ginger
4 fresh pears, cut in half, peeled and cored

Combine water and sugar and bring to a boil. Add lemon and ginger. Place pears in a baking dish. Pour syrup mixture over pears. Cover and bake in 350°F. oven 30-45 minutes or until tender. Turn once during baking period. Serve chilled for dessert or warm to accompany meat.

Orange Gelatin

Makes 4 servings

Calories: 95 per serving

1	tablespoon (1 envelope) unflavored gelatin
¼	cup cold water
¾	cup hot water
⅓	cup sugar

1	cup orange juice
1	tablespoon lemon juice
1	teaspoon grated orange rind, optional

Sprinkle gelatin over cold water in saucepan and allow to stand 5 minutes. Add hot water and sugar. Heat, stirring constantly until gelatin is dissolved. Remove from heat. Stir in remaining ingredients. Pour into 4 half-cup custard cups or a two-cup mold and chill until firm.
Variations: **Fruit Gelatin** – Chill gelatin until thickened to the consistency of unbeaten egg white. Stir in 1½ cups fresh or canned, drained, cut-up fruit. Chill until firm.
Orange Whip – Chill gelatin until thickened to the consistency of unbeaten egg white. Beat with rotary beater or electric mixer until light and foamy. Chill until firm. Serve with orange sections or fresh berries.

Apple Crisp

Makes 8 servings

Calories: 225 per serving

1½	pounds (5 medium) apples, sliced
2	tablespoons lemon juice
¼	teaspoon cinnamon
⅔	cup all-purpose flour

½	cup packed brown sugar
½	cup uncooked oatmeal
⅓	cup margarine*

Arrange apples in a lightly-oiled 2-quart casserole. Sprinkle with lemon juice and cinnamon. In a separate bowl, combine flour, brown sugar and oatmeal. Cut in margarine with a fork or pastry blender until mixture is crumbly. Spread over fruit. Bake in 375°F. oven 40 minutes or until apples are tender.
Variations: **Peach Crisp** – Use 1½ pounds (6 medium) sliced fresh peaches in place of apples.
Blueberry Crisp – Use 3 cups fresh or frozen blueberries in place of apples.

*See page 2

Lemon Sherbet

Makes 6 servings

Calories: 130 per serving

1½ teaspoons unflavored gelatin
2 tablespoons cold water
2 cups hot skim milk
¾ cup sugar

½ cup lemon juice
1 teaspoon grated lemon peel
1 egg white

Sprinkle gelatin over cold water in a saucepan and allow to stand 5 minutes. Add hot milk and sugar. Heat, stirring constantly until gelatin is dissolved. Chill until thickened to the consistency of unbeaten egg white. Gradually stir in lemon juice and lemon peel. Mixture will appear separated at this point. Place in a shallow pan in freezer until mixture is frozen at the edges. In a separate bowl, beat egg white until it forms soft peaks. Beat partially frozen lemon mixture until fluffy but not melted. Gently fold in egg white. Freeze until firm.

Strawberry Sherbet

Makes 6 servings

Calories: 155 per serving

1 tablespoon (1 envelope) unflavored gelatin
¼ cup cold water
1 cup hot water
½ cup sugar

2 packages (10 ounces each) frozen strawberries, thawed, or 2 cups sliced fresh strawberries, sweetened to taste, and allowed to stand 2 hours
3 tablespoons lemon juice

Sprinkle gelatin over cold water in saucepan and allow to stand 5 minutes. Add hot water and sugar. Heat, stirring constantly until gelatin is dissolved. Remove from heat and add undrained strawberries and lemon juice. Place in shallow pan in freezer until mixture is firm at the edges. Beat with electric mixer until well mixed. Return to freezer until firm. Variation: **Raspberry Sherbet** — Use fresh or frozen raspberries in place of strawberries.

Baked Custard

Makes 6 servings

Calories: 80 per serving

2½ cups skim milk
¼ cup sugar
4 egg whites
1 teaspoon vanilla

1 tablespoon table sherry
few drops yellow food coloring
dash nutmeg

Mix all ingredients together except nutmeg. Pour into lightly-oiled custard cups. Sprinkle with nutmeg. Place custard cups in pan of hot water and bake in 325°F. oven 50 minutes or until knife inserted near center of custard comes out clean.

Vanilla Pudding

Makes 5 servings

Calories: 165 per serving

⅓ cup sugar
¼ cup cornstarch
2¾ cups skim milk
2 tablespoons margarine*

1 teaspoon vanilla
3 drops yellow food coloring, optional

Combine sugar and cornstarch in a saucepan and mix well. Add 1 cup of milk and stir until sugar is dissolved and cornstarch is evenly dispersed. Stir in remaining milk. Bring to a boil over medium heat, stirring constantly. Boil 1 minute. Remove from heat. Stir in margarine, vanilla and yellow food coloring. Chill. May be served in parfait glasses layered with fresh strawberries or other fruit or as a filling for Matzo Crumb Pie Crust, page 99.

Variations: **Chocolate Pudding** – Increase sugar to ⅔ cup and add 3 tablespoons cocoa to sugar and cornstarch mixture. Omit yellow food coloring.
Butterscotch Pudding – Substitute brown sugar for white sugar. Increase margarine to 3 tablespoons. Omit yellow food coloring.

*See page 2

Fruit Rice Pudding

Makes 6 servings   Calories: 110 per serving

1¼   cups unsalted cooked rice
1   cup drained fruit cocktail

¼   cup maple syrup
1   tablespoon powdered sugar

Mix rice, fruit cocktail and maple syrup. Spoon into sauce dishes or small parfait glasses. Sprinkle with powdered sugar before serving.

Fresh Fruit Cobbler

Makes 6 servings   Calories: 280 per serving

3   cups fresh fruit (cherries, blueberries, blackberries, peaches or apricots)
¾   cup sugar
1   tablespoon cornstarch

1   cup boiling water
½   teaspoon cinnamon, optional
1   tablespoon margarine*
½   recipe Biscuits, page 73

Wash fruit and drain. Peel and slice peaches or apricots. In a saucepan, combine sugar and cornstarch and mix well. Pour boiling water gradually into sugar mixture, stirring constantly. Bring to a boil and add fruit. Pour into shallow 1½-quart baking dish. Sprinkle cinnamon over top and dot with margarine. Prepare biscuit dough and drop by spoonfuls on top of fruit. Bake in preheated 400°F.

oven 25-30 minutes until biscuits are done.

Variations: **Fruit Cobbler** – Use 3 cups drained canned fruit in place of fresh fruit. Reserve juice in which fruit was packed. Add cold water to make 1 cup. Omit sugar. Stir cornstarch into cold juice until dissolved. Cook until thickened, stirring constantly and combine with fruit. Proceed as directed above.

*See page 2

106

Brownies

Makes 12 brownies   Calories: 195 per brownie

¾   cup all-purpose flour
1   cup sugar
⅓   cup cocoa
½   teaspoon baking powder*

½   cup margarine*, melted
3   egg whites
1   teaspoon vanilla
½   cup chopped walnuts

Sift dry ingredients together into bowl. Add margarine, egg whites and vanilla and beat. Stir in nuts. Pour into a lightly-oiled 8-inch square baking pan. Bake in preheated 350°F. oven 30-35 minutes. Cool and cut into squares.

Spiced Fruit

Makes 8 servings   Calories: 285 per serving

1   cup firmly-packed brown sugar
½   cup sauterne wine
¼   cup cider vinegar
15 whole cloves
2   sticks cinnamon
⅛   teaspoon curry powder*
8   canned peach halves, drained

8   canned pear halves, drained
16 or more honeydew melon balls, fresh or frozen, or 2 kiwi fruit, pared and sliced
8   fresh pineapple spears or 1 can (20 ounces) pineapple chunks, drained

In a saucepan, combine brown sugar, wine, vinegar, cloves, cinnamon and curry powder. Heat through. Combine fruits in a bowl. Pour hot spiced syrup over fruits. Cool, then chill overnight. Remove cloves and cinnamon sticks. Serve alone or with ice milk or Mock Whipped Cream, page 108.

*See page 2

Chocolate Sauce

Makes 1 cup

Calories: 35 per tablespoon

3 tablespoons cocoa
½ cup sugar
⅓ cup skim milk

1 tablespoon margarine*, melted
1 teaspoon vanilla

Combine cocoa and sugar. Heat milk and margarine. Slowly add cocoa-sugar mixture, stirring constantly. Bring to boil, add vanilla. Mixture will thicken as it cools. Serve over angel food cake or ice milk.

Mock Whipped Cream

Makes 2 cups

Calories: 100 per 2 tablespoons

1½ cups (12 ounces) unsalted dry cottage cheese
½ cup tub margarine*

1 cup powdered sugar
2 teaspoons lemon juice
¼ teaspoon vanilla

Mix all ingredients together in a blender until smooth. Use as a topping for fresh fruit or other desserts. May be stored in refrigerator up to 1 week.

*See page 2

Happy Snacking

Happy Snacking

Snack foods can be satisfying and nutritious and still be compatible with the sodium and fat changes you have made in your diet if you select them carefully.

Fruits and raw vegetables are good examples of the kinds of snack foods recommended. They contain no sodium, fat or cholesterol and are low in calories which should please those who are watching their weight. On the other hand, snack foods such as potato and corn chips, chocolate candy, salty crackers, buttered popcorn and pizza contain salt and saturated fat and should be avoided.

There are many possible choices for appetizing snacks:
- Fruits and juices
- Raw vegetables served alone or with specially prepared dips, pages 84, 113 and 114
- Home-fried tortilla shells broken into chip-size pieces and served with specially prepared dips, pages 113 and 114
- Soda crackers without salt sprinkled on top, spread with peanut butter
- Skim milk, low-fat yogurt, low-fat frozen yogurt, sherbet or ice milk
- Cereal
- Bread sticks or unsalted pretzels
- Unsalted popcorn flavored with margarine
- Specially prepared homemade cookies and cakes
- Sandwiches, canapés or tea sandwiches
- Unsalted nuts or seeds, shelled or unshelled
- Plain hard candies

Many of the pre-packaged snack foods on your grocer's shelves contain added salt and are fried or prepared with saturated fat. Reading labels on the package is the best way to determine whether or not that particular food product is for you.

Fresh Vegetable Platter

green pepper strips
carrot sticks
cauliflower flowerets
radish roses
green onions
asparagus spears

cucumber slices, unpeeled
cherry tomatoes
fresh mushrooms
zucchini sticks, unpeeled
whole green beans
broccoli tips

Arrange an assortment of fresh vegetables on a platter. Serve with Cocktail Dip, page 114, California Onion Dip, page 113, Mock Sour Cream, page 84, or Swedish Dill Sauce, page 87.

Dill Pickles

Makes 1 quart

Calories: 45 per pickle

10-12 dill-size cucumbers
1 tablespoon dill seed or
   3 heads fresh dill
1 tablespoon whole pickling spice
2 garlic cloves

⅛ teaspoon alum
2 grape leaves, optional
2¼ cups water
1½ cups cider vinegar
1 tablespoon sugar

Wash cucumbers thoroughly. Soak overnight in cold water. Dry cucumbers and place in a clean, hot quart jar. Add dill, pickling spice, garlic, alum and grape leaves to the jar. Mix water, vinegar and sugar and bring to boil. Fill jar to within ½ inch of the top with boiling liquid. Wipe rim of jar, screw lid on tightly, and place in a Dutch oven or other deep pan. Cover jar completely with water. Bring to a boil and boil for 20 minutes (at higher altitudes longer processing is necessary). Store pickles 2 weeks before using. When cucumbers are plentiful, this recipe may be made in large quantities.

Bread and Butter Pickles

Makes 1 quart

Calories: 70 per ¼ cup

4	cups sliced cucumbers (approximately 8 medium)
2	medium onions, sliced in rings
1¼	cups cider vinegar
1¼	cups sugar
½	teaspoon turmeric
½	teaspoon mustard seed
¼	teaspoon celery seed

Combine cucumbers and onions and cover with crushed ice. Allow to stand 3 hours. Drain. Combine vinegar, sugar and spices and heat just to boiling. Add cucumber mixture and heat 2-3 minutes. Chill and serve. May be refrigerated for 1 month. For storage without refrigeration, sterilize 2 pint jars and immediately pack hot pickles loosely to within ½ inch of top. Wipe rim of jar, screw lid on tightly and place in a Dutch oven or other deep pan. Cover jars completely with water. Bring to boil and boil for 5 minutes (at higher altitudes, longer processing is necessary). When cucumbers are plentiful, this recipe may be made in larger quantities.

Variation: **Pickle Relish** — Finely chop the cucumbers and onions and add 1 finely-chopped green or red pepper. Cook until liquid in mixture is nearly gone and relish is thickened.

Sugared Peanuts

Makes 10 servings

Calories: 240 per serving

2	cups unsalted peanuts
1	cup sugar

½ cup water

Mix all ingredients together and place over medium heat, stirring occasionally. Cook until mixture crystallizes and coats peanuts, approximately 10-12 minutes. Spread on lightly-oiled cookie sheet. Bake in 300°F. oven 20-25 minutes, mixing occasionally. Cool and store in tightly-covered container.

Party Mix

Makes 14 servings

Calories: 85 per ¼ cup serving

¼ cup margarine*
½ teaspoon garlic powder
½ cup unsalted pretzels

½ cup puffed rice
1 cup spoon-size shredded wheat
½ cup unsalted peanuts

Melt margarine in skillet. Add garlic powder and mix. Add remaining ingredients and toss together. Serve warm.

May use walnuts, pecans or a mixture of nuts in place of peanuts. May also add ¼ cup raisins and omit garlic powder.

California Onion Dip

Makes 1¼ cups

Calories: 10 per tablespoon

¼ cup skim milk
2 unsalted beef bouillon cubes
1 cup (8 ounces) unsalted dry cottage cheese
2 teaspoons lemon juice
2 teaspoons vermouth or dry white

table wine
1 teaspoon onion powder
½ teaspoon garlic powder
2 tablespoons onion flakes or ¼ cup chopped green onion

Mix milk and bouillon cubes in blender until bouillon dissolves. Add remaining ingredients except onion and blend at high speed until smooth. Stir in onion. Use as

a dip for raw vegetables, toast strips or specially prepared tortilla shells, broken into pieces. See Taco recipe, page 39 for directions for preparing tortilla shells.

*See page 2

Cocktail Dip

Makes 1¼ cups

Calories: 10 per tablespoon

1 cup unsalted chili sauce
2 tablespoons lemon juice
4 drops Tabasco sauce

2 tablespoons grated fresh horseradish
½ teaspoon onion powder

Mix all ingredients together in a blender and chill. Use as sauce for crabmeat or clams or as a dip for raw vegetables.

Fudge

Makes 4 dozen pieces

Calories: 45 per piece

1 cup packed brown sugar
1 cup sugar
⅓ cup cocoa

⅔ cup skim milk
3 tablespoons margarine*
1 teaspoon vanilla

Mix brown sugar, sugar and cocoa in a 3-quart saucepan. Add milk and mix. Cook over medium heat until fudge reaches 236°F. on a candy thermometer or until a small amount of syrup dropped in cold water forms a soft ball. Remove from heat. Add margarine but do not stir. Cool until bottom of pan is lukewarm. Add vanilla and beat with an electric mixer 5-10 minutes or until fudge is thick and no longer glossy. Spread in lightly-oiled 8-inch square baking pan. Cool until firm and cut into squares.

Variations: **Nut Fudge** — After beating, stir in ½ cup chopped walnuts.

Peanut Butter Fudge — After beating, add ½ cup peanut butter*. Run a table knife through the fudge to form streaks.

See page 2

Spiced Nuts

Makes 10 servings

Calories: 200 per serving

1 egg white
⅔ cup sugar

1 teaspoon cinnamon
2 cups pecan halves

Beat egg white until foamy. Gradually add sugar and cinnamon and beat until egg white forms stiff peaks. Add pecans and stir until coated with mixture. Separate pecans with a fork and place on cookie sheet which has been greased with margarine. *Bake in 325°F. oven 15-20 minutes or until egg white is dry and slightly browned.

Fruit-Nut Snack Mix

Makes 12 ¼ cup servings

Calories: 155 per serving

½ cup dried apricots, cut in quarters
½ cup dates, cut in half
¼ cup raisins
½ cup whole almonds

½ cup walnut halves
½ cup unsalted peanuts
¼ cup unsalted sunflower seeds

Toss ingredients together. Store in tightly covered container. You may add your favorite dried fruits or nuts in place of those listed.

See page 2

Recipe Index

Calculated Food Values of Recipes[1]

Dash (—) denotes lack of reliable data. Parentheses ( ) indicate lack of complete data for one or more ingredients. Data should be interpreted as a minimum.

	Page	Calories	Carbo-hydrate gm.	Protein Total gm.	Protein Animal[2] gm.	Fat Total gm.	Fat Polyunsat.[3] F.A.-Linoleic gm.
BREADS							
Banana Bread 1 sl	75	130	21.1	2.1	.6	4.7	2.6
Biscuits 1 biscuit	73	130	15.6	2.5	.5	6.2	3.5
Blueberry Muffins 1 muffin	77	135	20.7	2.8	.9	4.8	2.7
Corn Muffins 1 muffin	73	150	24.5	4.5	1.9	3.8	2.0
Crepes 1 crepe	78	60	6.5	1.3	.6	2.8	1.0
Marmalade Coffee Cake—1 serving	76	290	51.0	4.2	1.2	8.3	4.7
Pancakes 1 pancake	77	90	11.9	2.3	1.1	3.8	2.1
Seasoned Croutons ¼ c	75	85	6.0	1.1	0	6.1	2.0
Streusel-Filled Coffee Cake—1 serving	74	295	44.6	4.2	1.2	11.5	4.9
White Bread 1 sl	71	75	14.4	2.3	.4	.9	.5
DESSERTS							
Angel Food Cake 1 serving	93	130	27.6	4.1	3.1	.1	.1
Apple Crisp 1 serving	103	225	37.0	2.0	0	8.6	2.9

[1] *Highland View Hospital — Case Western Reserve University Computerized Nutrient Data Base and selected other sources, May 1, 1977.*
[2] *From animal sources: meat, fish, poultry, milk, milk products, cheese, eggs.*
[3] *Values represent data for the significant sources of fat and cholesterol.*
[4] *Values obtained using special ingredients as denoted by asterisk in recipe.*
[5] *Values obtained using first ingredient listed when a choice is given.*

Sat. F.A.[3]	Choles-terol[3]	Calcium	Phosphorus	Iron	Sodium	Potassium[5]	Sodium[4]	Potassium[4,5]
gm.	mg.	mg.	mg.	mg.	mg.	mg.	mg.	mg.
.6	0	12	27	(.4)	58	93	9	142
.8	.3	37	56	(.6)	106	39	8	137
.6	.2	32	48	(.6)	96	49	13	130
.5	.6	58	86	(.8)	126	95	28	192
.5	.2	(12)	(15)	(.2)	42	24	5	24
1.1	.3	41	58	(.9)	86	88	21	153
.5	.5	46	(55)	(.3)	95	51	16	128
1.2	0	13	13	.3	128	17	4	16
1.8	.3	60	79	(1.2)	203	121	23	206
.1	.2	17	28	.5	7	37		
0	0	19	35	.3	42	91		
1.5	0	22	38	1.1	98	176	6	176

Calculated Food Values of Recipes[1]

Dash (—) denotes lack of reliable data. Parentheses ( ) indicate lack of complete data for one or more ingredients. Data should be interpreted as a minimum.

	Page	Calories	Carbo-hydrate gm.	Protein Total gm.	Protein Animal[2] gm.	Fat Total gm.	Fat Polyunsat.[3] F.A.-Linoleic gm.
DESSERTS (Continued)							
Apple-Filled Crepes 1 crepe	99	135	20.6	1.7	.7	5.7	2.0
Apple Pie ⅛ pie	101	450	70.8	4.4	.4	16.7	9.5
Applesauce Cake 1 serving	91	335	57.8	3.8	.7	10.7	3.8
Baked Custard 1 serving	105	80	13.6	5.9	5.9	.1	0
Baked Pears 1 serving	102	100	26.3	.4	0	.4	0
Brownies 1 serving	107	200	23.8	2.8	.8	11.1	4.3
Cherry Pie ⅛ pie	100	460	73.0	5.2	.4	17.4	9.5
Chocolate Cake with White Cream Frosting 1 serving	93	360	46.8	3.9	1.6	18.4	8.5
Chocolate Sauce 1 tbsp	108	35	7.0	.4	.2	1.0	.2
Citrus Chiffon 1 serving	102	70	16.3	1.9	1.7	.1	0
Date Rounds 1 cookie	96	80	9.6	.9	0	4.2	1.7
Denver Chocolate Pudding Cake- plain 1 serving	94	255	51.9	2.8	.5	5.3	1.5

[1] *Highland View Hospital — Case Western Reserve University Computerized Nutrient Data Base and selected other sources, May 1, 1977.*
[2] *From animal sources: meat, fish, poultry, milk, milk products, cheese, eggs.*
[3] *Values represent data for the significant sources of fat and cholesterol.*
[4] *Values obtained using special ingredients as denoted by asterisk in recipe.*
[5] *Values obtained using first ingredient listed when a choice is given.*

Sat. F.A.[3]	Choles-terol[3]	Calcium	Phosphorus	Iron	Sodium	Potassium[5]	Sodium[4]	Potassium[4,5]
gm.	mg.	mg.	mg.	mg.	mg.	mg.	mg.	mg.
1.0	.2	16	21	.3	74	90	11	90
2.3	.2	30	56	1.5	25	192	8	192
1.9	0	33	54	(1.3)	205	131	16	194
0	2.0	125	100	0	83	177		
0	0	11	13	.4	2	211		
2.1	0	15	49	.7	122	86	13	101
2.3	.2	37	57	1.5	26	199	9	199
3.1	.5	50	(78)	(.8)	213	100	23	184
.3	.1	8	(13)	.1	12	28	3	28
0	.6	39	32	0	16	98		
.7	0	6	(14)	.3	38	39	1	39
1.4	.3	53	(86)	(1.4)	146	161	12	246

Calculated Food Values of Recipes[1]

Dash (—) denotes lack of reliable data. Parentheses ( ) indicate lack of complete data for one or more ingredients. Data should be interpreted as a minimum.

DESSERTS (Continued)	Page	Calories	Carbo-hydrate gm.	Protein Total gm.	Protein Animal[2] gm.	Fat Total gm.	Fat Polyunsat.[3] F.A.-Linoleic gm.
Fresh Fruit Cobbler, Cherry 1 serving	106	285	51.1	3.3	.5	8.1	4.1
Fruit Rice Pudding 1 serving	106	110	26.8	1.0	0	.1	0
Lemon Nut Cookies 1 cookie	94	90	9.1	1.2	.3	5.5	2.2
Lemon Sherbet 1 serving	104	130	29.8	3.8	3.7	.1	0
Matzo Crumb Pie Crust ⅛ crust	99	135	19.6	1.7	0	5.9	2.0
Mock Whipped Cream 2 tbsp	108	100	8.2	4.0	4.0	5.8	2.0
Oatmeal Cookies 1 cookie	95	75	9.8	1.0	0	3.3	1.2
Orange Gelatin 1 serving	103	95	22.8	2.0	1.5	.1	0
Peanut Butter Cookies 1 cookie	95	75	7.9	1.8	.1	4.5	1.4
Pie Crust ⅛ crust	100	260	25.4	3.8	.4	15.6	9.0
Pineapple Upside-Down Cake, 1 serving	91	365	54.2	3.2	.8	15.7	5.8
Popcorn Macaroons 1 macaroon	98	21	2.6	.4	.2	1.1	.6
Pralines 1 praline	97	55	5.1	.5	.1	3.7	1.2
Pumpkin Pie ⅛ pie	101	255	39.8	7.2	5.0	8.1	4.5

[1] Highland View Hospital – Case Western Reserve University Computerized Nutrient Data Base and selected other sources, May 1, 1977.
[2] From animal sources: meat, fish, poultry, milk, milk products, cheese, eggs.
[3] Values represent data for the significant sources of fat and cholesterol.
[4] Values obtained using special ingredients as denoted by asterisk in recipe.
[5] Values obtained using first ingredient listed when a choice is given.

Sat.F.A.[3] gm.	Choles-terol[3] mg.	Calcium mg.	Phosphorus mg.	Iron mg.	Sodium mg.	Potassium[5] mg.	Sodium[4] mg.	Potassium[4,5] mg.
1.1	.3	50	65	(.8)	130	148	9	245
0	0	21	17	.7	4	95		
.9	10.1	6	(18)	.3	49	22.5	3	21
0	1.6	101	80	.1	44	149		
1.1	0	2	1	0	70	(2)	7	(2)
1.0	0	7	40	.1	70	6	2	5
.6	0	6	(17)	.4	39	29	2	29
0	0	7	10	.1	3	122		
.8	5.0	9	29	.3	66	47	2	55
2.0	.2	17	38	.9	6	45		
2.9	0	41	47	1.3	278	159	19	229
.1	0	2	(7)	.1	2	10		
.6	3.4	5	(9)	.2	33	24	3	24
1.0	2.1	161	131	1.3	212	361	78	361

Calculated Food Values of Recipes[1]

Dash (—) denotes lack of reliable data. Parentheses ( ) indicate lack of complete data for one or more ingredients. Data should be interpreted as a minimum.

	Page	Calories	Carbo-hydrate gm.	Protein Total gm.	Protein Animal[2] gm.	Fat Total gm.	Fat Polyunsat.[3] F.A.-Linoleic gm.
DESSERTS (Continued)							
Spiced Fruit 1 serving	107	285	74.7	1.0	0	.5	0
Strawberry Sherbet 1 serving	104	155	38.7	1.4	1.0	.2	0
Sunshine Crepes 1 crepe	98	200	29.9	2.1	.7	9.2	3.3
Vanilla Cookies 1 cookie	97	70	7.1	.9	.2	4.0	1.4
Vanilla Pudding 1 serving	105	165	25.4	4.9	4.9	4.7	1.6
Walnut Cocoons 1 cocoon	96	95	8.2	1.4	0	6.6	2.9
White Cake with White Cream Frosting 1 serving	92	415	53.1	4.5	1.9	20.8	8.6

ENTREES & ACCOMPANIMENTS

BEEF							
Beef Bourguignon 1 serving	21	210	15.6	19.7	17.5	7.3	1.9
Beef Stroganoff 1 serving	23	265	11.2	20.9	18.2	15.0	4.9

[1] *Highland View Hospital — Case Western Reserve University Computerized Nutrient Data Base and selected other sources, May 1, 1977.*
[2] *From animal sources: meat, fish, poultry, milk, milk products, cheese, eggs.*
[3] *Values represent data for the significant sources of fat and cholesterol.*
[4] *Values obtained using special ingredients as denoted by asterisk in recipe.*
[5] *Values obtained using first ingredient listed when a choice is given.*

	Choles-terol[3]	Calcium	Phosphorus	Iron	Sodium	Potassium[5]	Sodium[4]	Potassium[4,5]
Sat. F.A.[3] gm.	mg.	mg.	mg.	mg.	mg.	mg.	mg.	mg.
0	0	47	31	1.9	16	466		
0	0	13	16	.6	3	110		
1.7	.2	22	26	.4	122	176	13	176
.7	5.0	3	(9)	.2	49	10	3	10
.8	2.7	164	(129)	0	126	197	71	197
1.0	0	6	(23)	.3	47	27	1	27
3.3	.6	62	(79)	.7	267	83	30	178
2.1	52.2	37	136	3.1	50	574		
3.8	54.1	39	227	3.0	60	983		

Calculated Food Values of Recipes[1]

Dash (—) denotes lack of reliable data. Parentheses ( ) indicate lack of complete data for one or more ingredients. Data should be interpreted as a minimum.

BEEF (Continued)	Page	Calories	Carbo-hydrate gm.	Protein Total gm.	Protein Animal[2] gm.	Fat Total gm.	Fat Polyunsat.[3] F.A.-Linoleic gm.
Chili 1 serving	24	205	23.4	20.7	14.0	3.5	.1
Fantastic Beef Goulash 1 serving	25	225	29.7	19.6	14.0	3.3	.1
Fiesta Beef-Macaroni Casserole, 1 serving	26	260	32.7	26.0	20.9	2.8	.1
Marinated Beef Slices 1 serving	22	230	6.0	23.5	22.3	12.3	4.1
Meatloaf 1 serving	25	135	8.8	17.1	15.9	3.1	.1
Miniature Meatballs 6 meatballs	24	280	19.4	24.2	21.0	11.6	4.2
Peppered Roast Beef 1 serving	22	160	1.6	23.5	23.3	6.1	1.1
Rolled Flank Steak with Bread Dressing 1 serving	23	330	15.9	24.5	23.2	18.7	7.4
Sloppy Joes 1 serving	39	240	27.8	19.5	15.7	5.5	.5
Spaghetti with Meat Sauce, 1 serving	40	270	39.1	20.3	14.0	3.6	.1
Tacos 3 tacos	39	315	40.8	27.1	21.0	5.9	.2

[1] *Highland View Hospital — Case Western Reserve University Computerized Nutrient Data Base and selected other sources, May 1, 1977.*
[2] *From animal sources: meat, fish, poultry, milk, milk products, cheese, eggs.*
[3] *Values represent data for the significant sources of fat and cholesterol.*
[4] *Values obtained using special ingredients as denoted by asterisk in recipe.*
[5] *Values obtained using first ingredient listed when a choice is given.*

Sat.F.A.[3]	Choles-terol[3]	Calcium	Phosphorus	Iron	Sodium	Potassium[5]	Sodium[4]	Potassium[4,5]
gm.	mg.	mg.	mg.	mg.	mg.	mg.	mg.	mg.
1.2	40.7	50	244	4.8	157	843	45	843
1.2	40.7	(32)	(228)	(3.8)	61	(671)		
.9	30.5	48	279	(3.9)	44	624		
3.1	63.0	25	217	3.3	48	463		
1.3	41.1	47	162	2.1	95	315	72	319
2.8	61.0	45	235	4.7	141	696	82	696
2.2	67.7	15	204	2.8	50	310		
4.1	69.2	31	135	3.4	115	404	80	389
1.8	45.7	44	182	2.9	237	304	41	304
1.2	40.7	43	227	4.5	214	829	45	819
1.8	61.0	170	333	5.9	(59)	(846)	(55)	846

Calculated Food Values of Recipes[1]

Dash(—) denotes lack of reliable data. Parentheses ( ) indicate lack of complete data for one or more ingredients. Data should be interpreted as a minimum.

CHICKEN	Page	Calories	Carbo-hydrate gm.	Protein Total gm.	Protein Animal[2] gm.	Fat Total gm.	Fat Polyunsat.[3] F.A.-Linoleic gm.
Chicken À L' Orange 1 serving	30	375	29.4	33.8	30.9	13.5	4.4
Chicken Cacciatore 1 serving	32	235	6.5	26.8	25.5	10.9	4.5
Chicken Italiano 1 serving	30	350	12.8	33.2	31.0	17.8	6.5
Golden Baked Chicken 1 serving	32	280	.9	31.1	30.9	16.5	5.5
Lemon-Baked Chicken 1 serving	31	302	1.5	31.1	30.9	18.6	9.1
Lemon-Barbecued Chicken 1 serving	29	255	19.2	31.6	31.1	5.4	1.3
FISH[6]							
Herbed Fillet of Sole 1 serving	35	165	1.8	23.7	23.5	6.9	2.0
Oven-Fried Fish 1 serving	36	300	4.6	25.4	24.5	19.7	8.2
Poached Salmon Steaks 1 serving	33	185	7.1	24.8	24.4	5.9	—
Rolled Fish Fillets 1 serving	34	115	.5	24.5	24.5	1.1	0
Tomato Crown Fish 1 serving	33	155	6.1	24.5	23.3	3.1	1.3

[1] *Highland View Hospital – Case Western Reserve University Computerized Nutrient Data Base and selected other sources, May 1, 1977.*
[2] *From animal sources: meat, fish, poultry, milk, milk products, cheese, eggs.*
[3] *Values represent data for the significant sources of fat and cholesterol.*
[4] *Values obtained using special ingredients as denoted by asterisk in recipe.*
[5] *Values obtained using first ingredient listed when a choice is given.*
[6] *Values for fresh fish or for frozen fish which has not been processed with salt.*

Sat.F.A.[3]	Choles- terol[3]	Calcium	Phosphorus	Iron	Sodium	Potassium[5]	Sodium[4]	Potassium[4,5]
gm.	mg.	mg.	mg.	mg.	mg.	mg.	mg.	mg.
2.8	87.8	39	307	2.6	82	650		
2.0	63.2	27	245	1.6	57	579		
4.1	87.8	42	284	2.5	304	427	112	426
4.0	87.8	17	260	1.6	218	402	79	400
3.6	88.0	18	260	1.7	78	419		
1.9	88.3	16	273	1.8	79	422		
1.3	39.2	23	274	1.2	134	496	53	495
3.2	40.9	31	293	1.4	244	504	76	502
—	39.7	296	409	1.0	—	—	69	469
.2	40.9	19	282	1.2	—	—	64	488
.4	40.9	40	245	1.3	75	484	55	484

Calculated Food Values of Recipes[1]

Dash (—) denotes lack of reliable data. Parentheses ( ) indicate lack of complete data for one or more ingredients. Data should be interpreted as a minimum.

FISH[6] (Continued)	Page	Calories	Carbo-hydrate gm.	Protein Total gm.	Protein Animal[2] gm.	Fat Total gm.	Fat Polyunsat.[3] F.A.-Linoleic gm.
Tuna-Macaroni Casserole 1 serving	34	305	32.5	19.7	15.1	10.3	4.0
Tuna Oriental 1 serving	35	185	20.7	18.2	17.2	3.7	1.7
LAMB							
Lamb Curry 1 serving	36	155	3.2	16.3	15.8	8.4	1.5
PORK							
Hungarian Pork Chops 1 serving	28	150	3.0	14.5	14.3	8.5	1.2
Mediterranean Pork Chops 1 serving	29	125	.2	12.9	12.9	7.6	1.2
Pork Sausage Patties 1 patty	28	125	.5	14.5	14.5	6.7	.5
VEAL							
Lemon Veal with Spinach, 1 serving	27	240	6.6	29.2	26.7	11.1	4.0
Veal À L' Orange 1 serving	26	205	9.8	25.2	24.6	6.9	1.3

[1] *Highland View Hospital — Case Western Reserve University Computerized Nutrient Data Base and selected other sources, May 1, 1977.*
[2] *From animal sources: meat, fish, poultry, milk, milk products, cheese, eggs.*
[3] *Values represent data for the significant sources of fat and cholesterol.*
[4] *Values obtained using special ingredients as denoted by asterisk in recipe.*
[5] *Values obtained using first ingredient listed when a choice is given.*
[6] *Values for fresh fish or for frozen fish which has not been processed with salt.*

Sat.F.A.[3]	Choles-terol[3]	Calcium	Phosphorus	Iron	Sodium	Potassium[5]	Sodium[4]	Potassium[4,5]
gm.	mg.	mg.	mg.	mg.	mg.	mg.	mg.	mg.
1.5	30.3	104	213	2.2	206	371	65	368
.4	38.7	(32)	(138)	(1.6)	32	388		
1.7	59.0	14	137	1.7	59	203	43	193
2.9	40.2	62	179	1.8	49	246		
2.5	37.0	10	137	1.8	28	168		
2.2	40.8	(13)	(146)	(1.9)	43	201	42	201
1.4	74.2	96	253	5.0	74	672		
.8	71.3	24	200	3.3	48	475		

Calculated Food Values of Recipes[1]

Dash (—) denotes lack of reliable data. Parentheses ( ) indicate lack of complete data for one or more ingredients. Data should be interpreted as a minimum.

	Page	Calories	Carbo-hydrate gm.	Protein Total gm.	Protein Animal[2] gm.	Fat Total gm.	Fat Polyunsat.[3] F.A.-Linoleic gm.
VEAL (Continued)							
Veal Curry 1 serving	27	195	3.7	27.2	26.9	6.9	1.1
MISCELLANEOUS							
Baked Beans 1 serving	38	180	33.4	9.2	2.1	1.7	.1
Bread Dressing 1 serving	31	220	22.0	2.0	0	14.6	7.8
Cheese Blintzes 1 blintz	38	80	8.9	5.2	4.5	2.9	1.0
French Toast 1 sl	37	150	13.0	5.5	3.5	8.1	3.1
Fried Rice 1 serving	41	210	24.6	5.8	3.5	9.8	5.4
No-Cholesterol Egg Substitute 1 recipe	37	200	3.2	14.9	14.9	13.6	7.8
Seasoned Rice 1 serving	41	280	31.4	3.2	.2	15.9	5.6
Spaghetti with Mushroom Sauce 1 serving	40	225	36.7	5.8	0	6.5	2.1

[1] *Highland View Hospital — Case Western Reserve University Computerized Nutrient Data Base and selected other sources, May 1, 1977.*
[2] *From animal sources: meat, fish, poultry, milk, milk products, cheese, eggs.*
[3] *Values represent data for the significant sources of fat and cholesterol.*
[4] *Values obtained using special ingredients as denoted by asterisk in recipe.*
[5] *Values obtained using first ingredient listed when a choice is given.*

Sat.F.A.[3] gm.	Choles-terol[3] mg.	Calcium mg.	Phosphorus mg.	Iron mg.	Sodium mg.	Potassium[5] mg.	Sodium[4] mg.	Potassium[4,5] mg.
1.1	74.9	13	218	3.6	84	408	41	408
.4	6.2	64	159	2.9	20	534		
1.9	0	28	30	.7	103	152	51	160
.5	.2	18	52	(.2)	46	32	12	31
1.4	.4	49	(47)	.6	220	92	54	92
1.4	9.9	16	67	1.3	27	132	24	130
1.7	.9	66	61	.1	203	246		
2.8	0	27	45	1.2	194	682	12	680
1.1	0	28	107	2.5	184	558	18	557

Calculated Food Values of Recipes[1]

Dash (—) denotes lack of reliable data. Parentheses ( ) indicate lack of complete data for one or more ingredients. Data should be interpreted as a minimum.

SALAD & SALAD DRESSINGS	Page	Calories	Carbo-hydrate gm.	Protein Total gm.	Protein Animal[2] gm.	Fat Total gm.	Fat Polyunsat.[3] F.A.-Linoleic gm.
SALADS Ambrosia 1 serving	61	125	28.5	3.8	2.8	.2	
Macaroni Salad 1 serving	64	220	26.3	3.6	0	11.4	5.5
Marinated Tomato Slices—1 serving	62	85	5.4	1.2	0	7.0	3.9
Orange-Grapefruit Salad—1 serving	63	145	22.0	1.6	0	7.1	3.9
Pineapple Coleslaw 1 serving	61	150	19.1	.9	0	8.9	4.4
Potato Salad 1 serving	63	220	19.7	2.9	.3	14.9	7.3
Three Bean Salad 1 serving	62	185	19.4	2.7	0	11.8	6.7
Waldorf Salad 1 serving	61	210	14.2	1.1	0	17.8	8.8
SALAD DRESSINGS Basic Salad Dressing 1 tbsp	64	80	.4	0	0	9.1	5.2
Blender Mayonnaise 1 tbsp	67	125	.2	.2	.2	13.9	7.8
Italian Dressing 1 tbsp	65	65	.5	0	0	7.3	4.2

[1] *Highland View Hospital — Case Western Reserve University Computerized Nutrient Data Base and selected other sources, May 1, 1977.*
[2] *From animal sources: meat, fish, poultry, milk, milk products, cheese, eggs.*
[3] *Values represent data for the significant sources of fat and cholesterol.*
[4] *Values obtained using special ingredients as denoted by asterisk in recipe.*
[5] *Values obtained using first ingredient listed when a choice is given.*

Sat. F.A.[3] gm.	Choles-terol[3] mg.	Calcium mg.	Phosphorus mg.	Iron mg.	Sodium mg.	Potassium[5] mg.	Sodium[4] mg.	Potassium[4,5] mg.
	.1	30	(50)	(.7)	10	216		
1.9	9.6	(16)	(57)	(1.0)	93	115	14	137
.9	0	16	29	.6	4	245		
.9	0	57	40	.9	4	353		
1.5	7.7	(28)	(17)	(.5)	73	170	9	187
2.6	12.9	(36)	(68)	(1.0)	137	415	30	442
1.5	0	27	51	1.0	3	181		
2.8	12.8	13	29	.4	117	146	10	174
1.2	0	0	1	0	0	5		
1.8	15.7	(2)	(6)	(.1)	1	3		
.9	0	1	1	0	0	8		

Calculated Food Values of Recipes[1]

Dash (—) denotes lack of reliable data. Parentheses ( ) indicate lack of complete data for one or more ingredients. Data should be interpreted as a minimum.

SALAD DRESSINGS (Continued)	Page	Calories	Carbo-hydrate gm.	Protein		Fat	
				Total gm.	Animal[2] gm.	Total gm.	Polyunsat.[3] F.A.-Linoleic gm.
Lemon-Poppy Seed Dressing 1 tbsp	65	55	10.4	.1	0	1.8	1.0
Russian Dressing 1 tbsp	65	65	.7	.1	0	7.3	4.2
Thousand Island Dressing-1 tbsp.	66	55	2.1	.3	0	5.5	2.7
Tomato French Dressing-1 tbsp.	64	70	1.3	.1	—	7.3	4.2
Vinaigrette Dressing 1 tbsp	66	55	.7	.4	.3	6.0	3.4
SANDWICH FILLINGS Chicken-Pineapple Salad-1 serving	45	175	7.7	14.2	13.9	9.6	4.2
Chicken-Pineapple Salad Sandwich 1 serving, 2 sl bread	45	300	30.9	18.2	14.0	11.1	4.2
Chicken Salad 1 serving	45	215	.9	14.2	13.9	16.9	7.9
Chicken Salad Sandwich 1 serving, 2 sl bread	45	335	24.1	18.2	14.0	18.4	7.9
Deviled Beef Spread 1 serving	46	165	6.1	18.0	17.2	7.2	2.0
Deviled Beef Spread Sandwich 1 serving, 2 sl bread	46	285	29.3	22.0	17.3	8.7	2.0

[1] *Highland View Hospital — Case Western Reserve University Computerized Nutrient Data Base and selected other sources, May 1, 1977.*
[2] *From animal sources: meat, fish, poultry, milk, milk products, cheese, eggs.*
[3] *Values represent data for the significant sources of fat and cholesterol.*
[4] *Values obtained using special ingredients as denoted by asterisk in recipe.*
[5] *Values obtained using first ingredient listed when a choice is given.*

Sat. F.A.[3]	Choles-terol[3]	Calcium	Phosphorus	Iron	Sodium	Potassium[5]	Sodium[4]	Potassium[4,5]
gm.	mg.	mg.	mg.	mg.	mg.	mg.	mg.	mg.
.2	0	3	2	.1	1	11		
.9	0	(1)	(2)	(.1)	1	20		
1.0	4.8	3	6	(.1)	43	33	3	44
.9	0	(1)	(3)	(.1)	1	34		
.8	.1	(3)	(3)	(0)	5	15		
2.1	46.1	12	120	.9	90	217	37	231
2.6	46.1	51	165	2.1	323	265	51	305
3.4	52.5	13	124	.8	157	213	50	241
3.9	52.5	52	169	2.0	390	261	64	315
2.1	53.3	17	164	2.3	74	317	48	324
2.6	53.3	55	209	3.5	307	365	61	398

137

Calculated Values of Recipes[1]

Dash (—) denotes lack of reliable data. Parentheses ( ) indicate lack of complete data for one or more ingredients. Data should be interpreted as a minimum.

SANDWICH FILLINGS (Continued)	Page	Calories	Carbo-hydrate gm.	Protein		Fat	
				Total gm.	Animal[2] gm.	Total gm.	Polyunsat.[3] F.A.-Linoleic gm.
Mock Cream Cheese 1/4 c	46	120	.4	8.4	8.3	9.3	3.2
Mock Cream Cheese Sandwich - 1 serving, 2 sl bread	46	245	23.6	12.4	8.4	10.8	3.2
Tuna Salad 1 serving	46	180	1.1	17.5	17.2	11.5	5.5
Tuna Salad Sandwich 1 serving - 2 sl bread	46	305	24.3	21.5	17.3	13.0	5.5
SNACKS Bread and Butter Pickles - 1/4 c	112	70	18.3	.4	0	.1	—
California Onion Dip 1 tbsp	113	15	1.1	(2.4)	(2.2)	(.1)	—
Cocktail Dip 1 tbsp	114	10	2.7	(.3)	(0)	0	—
Dill Pickles 1 sm	111	15	4.0	1.6	0	.3	0
Fruit-Nut Snack Mix 1/4 c	115	155	14.8	4.4	0	10.0	3.4
Fudge 1 pc	114	45	9.1	.3	.1	.9	.2
Party Mix 1/4 c	113	85	6.5	2.1	0	6.0	1.7
Spiced Nuts 1 serving	115	200	16.1	2.4	.3	15.4	3.7
Sugared Peanuts 1 serving	112	240	25.0	7.5	0	14.0	2.6

[1] *Highland View Hospital – Case Western Reserve University Computerized Nutrient Data Base and selected other sources, May 1, 1977.*
[2] *From animal sources: meat, fish, poultry, milk, milk products, cheese, eggs.*
[3] *Values represent data for the significant sources of fat and cholesterol.*
[4] *Values obtained using special ingredients as denoted by asterisk in recipe.*
[5] *Values obtained using first ingredient listed when a choice is given.*

Sat. F.A.[3]	Choles-terol[3]	Calcium	Phosphorus	Iron	Sodium	Potassium[5]	Sodium[4]	Potassium[4,5]
gm.	mg.	mg.	mg.	mg.	mg.	mg.	mg.	mg.
1.7	—	13	83	—	115	10	4	9
2.2	—	52	128	(1.2)	348	58	17	83
1.9	48.3	17	126	1.1	108	215	29	236
2.4	48.3	55	170	2.3	342	263	42	310
—	0	11	13	.3	4	97		
—	.1	8	25	0	5	128		
—	0	3	6	.1	3	43		
0	0	52	48	1.9	11	(281)		
1.1	0	34	106	1.3	4	253		
.2	.1	9	9	.2	12	33	3	33
1.0	0	10	39	.4	47	54	8	53
1.3	0	19	63	.5	7	136		
2.0	0	21	117	.7	2	203		

Calculated Food Values of Recipes[1]

Dash (—) denotes lack of reliable data. Parentheses ( ) indicate lack of complete data for one or more ingredients. Data should be interpreted as a minimum.

SOUPS AND SAUCES	Page	Calories	Carbo-hydrate gm.	Protein Total gm.	Protein Animal[2] gm.	Fat Total gm.	Fat Polyunsat.[3] F.A.-Linoleic gm.
SOUPS							
Beef Broth 1 c	81	10	2.2	2.0	0	.2	0
Chicken Broth 1 c	82	15	3.4	(.6)	0	.1	—
Cream of Asparagus Soup—1 serving	81	135	10.8	4.9	2.9	7.9	2.8
Hamburger-Vegetable Soup—1 serving	83	170	17.2	18.9	15.7	3.5	.1
Onion Soup 1 serving	83	185	14.7	2.6	0	12.9	5.4
Split Pea Soup 1 serving	82	75	14.5	5.2	0	.1	—
SAUCES							
Barbecue Sauce ¼ c	87	60	10.5	1.1	0	2.0	1.0
Catsup 1 tbsp	84	20	3.5	.3	0	.4	.1
Chili Powder 1 tsp	85	10	1.3	.3	0	.2	—
Chili Sauce 1 tbsp	85	20	4.3	(.4)	0	.5	.2
Chunky Tomato Sauce—¼ c	86	80	5.7	1.1	0	5.9	2.2
Herbed Margarine 1 tbsp	88	100	0	.1	0	11.5	4.2

[1] *Highland View Hospital — Case Western Reserve University Computerized Nutrient Data Base and selected other sources, May 1, 1977.*
[2] *From animal sources: meat, fish, poultry, milk, milk products, cheese, eggs.*
[3] *Values represent data for the significant sources of fat and cholesterol.*
[4] *Values obtained using special ingredients as denoted by asterisk in recipe.*
[5] *Values obtained using first ingredient listed when a choice is given.*

Sat. F.A.[3]	Choles-terol[3]	Calcium	Phosphorus	Iron	Sodium	Potassium[5]	Sodium[4]	Potassium[4,5]
gm.	mg.	mg.	mg.	mg.	mg.	mg.	mg.	mg.
0	0	11	83	.7	34	163		
—	—	(17)	(14)	(.4)	(6)	(63)		
1.4	1.6	117	116	.6	137	249	45	248
1.4	45.7	44	206	3.3	87	677	42	598
2.1	0	28	34	.6	157	885	27	884
—	0	29	85	1.5	24	267		
.2	0	14	24	1.1	23	252	11	252
.1	0	4	7	.3	9	79	5	79
—	0	9	6	.6	1	48		
.1	0	4	8	.4	9	93	3	93
1.1	0	7	17	.4	149	146	3	145
2.1	0	4	3	0	140	6	2	4

Calculated Food Values of Recipes[1]

Dash (—) denotes lack of reliable data. Parentheses ( ) indicate lack of complete data for one or more ingredients. Data should be interpreted as a minimum.

SAUCES (Continued)	Page	Calories	Carbo-hydrate gm.	Protein Total gm.	Protein Animal[2] gm.	Fat Total gm.	Fat Polyunsat.[3] F.A.-Linoleic gm.
Horseradish Sauce 1 tbsp	85	5	1.4	.2	0	0	—
Hot Prepared Mustard—1 tbsp	88	35	6.3	.8	0	.5	0
Lemon-Parsley Sauce—1 tbsp	86	75	.7	.1	0	8.4	3.0
Mock Sour Cream 1 tbsp	84	10	.3	2.1	2.1	0	—
Mushroom Sauce 1 tbsp	88	20	1.4	.8	.6	1.5	.6
Swedish Dill Sauce 1 serving	87	45	5.5	2.6	2.1	1.4	0
Tomato Sauce ¼ c	86	20	4.6	(.8)	(0)	.1	—
VEGETABLES Baked Tomatoes 1 serving	55	45	3.0	.7	0	3.5	2.0
Boiled Greens 1 serving	51	145	5.7	1.5	0	13.8	7.8
Broccoli Western Style—1 serving	50	185	4.9	2.6	0	18.3	10.4
Dilled Summer Squash 1 serving	55	40	3.1	.9	0	3.0	1.0
Eggplant Mexicana 1 serving	51	30	6.6	1.5	0	.3	—

[1] *Highland View Hospital – Case Western Reserve University Computerized Nutrient Data Base and selected other sources, May 1, 1977.*
[2] *From animal sources: meat, fish, poultry, milk, milk products, cheese, eggs.*
[3] *Values represent data for the significant sources of fat and cholesterol.*
[4] *Values obtained using special ingredients as denoted by asterisk in recipe.*
[5] *Values obtained using first ingredient listed when a choice is given.*

Sat. F.A.[3] gm.	Choles-terol[3] mg.	Calcium mg.	Phosphorus mg.	Iron mg.	Sodium mg.	Potassium[5] mg.	Sodium[4] mg.	Potassium[4,5] mg.
—	0	9	5	.1	3	44		
0	0	5	13	.2	0	19		
1.5	0	4	3	0	102	8	1	8
—	.1	7	23	0	3	8		
.3	.3	20	24	.1	27	55	9	54
.6	4.9	(97)	(69)	(.2)	33	143		
—	0	7	17	.8	9	200		
.4	0	11	17	.4	2	155		
1.7	0	(69)	(23)	(.9)	12	143		
2.3	0	37	49	.7	9	197		
.5	0	28	24	.4	36	134	1	133
—	0	13	31	.8	101	275	5	275

Calculated Food Values of Recipes[1]

Dash (—) denotes lack of reliable data. Parentheses ( ) indicate lack of complete data for one or more ingredients. Data should be interpreted as a minimum.

VEGETABLES (Continued)	Page	Calories	Carbo-hydrate gm.	Protein Total gm.	Protein Animal[2] gm.	Fat Total gm.	Fat Polyunsat.[3] F.A.-Linoleic gm.
Fried Cabbage with Noodles — 1 serving	49	130	18.4	3.4	1.8	5.0	2.3
Gingered Carrots 1 serving	49	105	5.9	.7	0	9.4	3.4
Green Beans and Corn—1 serving	52	70	10.3	1.9	0	3.2	1.0
Hash-Browned Potatoes — 1 serving	55	245	18.4	2.4	0	18.3	10.4
Potatoes O'Brien 1 serving	54	145	22.2	3.2	0	5.7	3.1
Potato Pancakes 1 serving	57	95	7.3	1.8	.8	6.9	3.9
Sauteed Cauliflower 1 serving	50	75	2.5	1.3	0	6.9	3.9
Sauteed Mushrooms on Toast — 1 serving	53	180	19.0	5.5	0	9.7	3.2
Scalloped Potatoes 1 serving	54	195	26.5	6.5	3.5	7.2	2.6
Scalloped Sweet Potatoes — 1 serving	56	185	31.9	1.3	0	6.3	2.0
Stuffed Green Peppers — 1 serving	53	130	15.4	3.2	0	6.6	2.2
Stuffed Mushrooms 1 serving	57	145	7.8	7.4	5.2	9.8	3.4
Sweet Potato Casserole — 1 serving	56	150	28.0	2.1	0	3.7	1.4
Sweet and Sour Green Beans — 1 serving	52	40	7.8	1.2	0	1.1	.3

[1] *Highland View Hospital — Case Western Reserve University Computerized Nutrient Data Base and selected other sources, May 1, 1977.*
[2] *From animal sources: meat, fish, poultry, milk, milk products, cheese, eggs.*
[3] *Values represent data for the significant sources of fat and cholesterol.*
[4] *Values obtained using special ingredients as denoted by asterisk in recipe.*
[5] *Values obtained using first ingredient listed when a choice is given.*

Sat. F.A.[3] gm.	Choles-terol[3] mg.	Calcium mg.	Phosphorus mg.	Iron mg.	Sodium mg.	Potassium[5] mg.	Sodium[4] mg.	Potassium[4,5] mg.
1.1	22	27	54	.8	55	119	9	119
1.7	0	28	24	.5	135	166	24	164
.5	0	23	46	.6	38	143	3	143
2.3	0	8	53	.6	3	530		
.7	0	21	70	.9	9	560		
.9	0	20	42	(.3)	49	136	12	172
.9	0	(15)	(26)	(.5)	7	223		
1.8	0	35	165	1.6	241	538	27	538
1.3	2.0	133	155	.8	139	631	56	631
1.1	0	28	36	.6	77	214	8	214
1.2	0	35	56	1.3	(162)	329	(34)	329
2.0	14.9	20	113	1.0	158	314	24	314
.5	0	36	57	.8	34	274	10	274
.2	0	30	24	.5	13	114	1	114